KEEPING THE BALANCE

CONTINUING THE STORY OF WOMEN IN TWENTIETH CENTURY COVENTRY

BY

THE WOMEN'S RESEARCH GROUP

The following members have contributed to this book:
Jean Appleton
Angela Atkin
Christine Bromley
Janet Done
June Hill
Margaret Hobley
Lynn Hockton
Janet Jonas
Dorothy Parker

Other titles by The Women's Research Group
Redress The Balance
Hurdy Gurdy Days
Telling Tales
All In A Day's Work

Published by:
The Women's Research Group

First Edition 2001
Reprinted 2007

Cover photographs are of:
Winifred Merrick Barrow
Antonia Hockton

© Copyright 2001 The Women's Research Group

ISBN 0-9540604-1-5

Printed by V & J System Printers, Hearsall Lane, Coventry

INTRODUCTION

Following 'Redressing The Balance' and 'Hurdy Gurdy Days', this book, 'Keeping the Balance' continues to celebrate the achievements of Coventry women in the twentieth century. The group which has produced this collection of profiles wish to reveal the extraordinary stories of ordinary women to show that their history, long overlooked, is absorbing, compelling and above all important in our understanding of the world around us.

In this volume, as in the previous two books, the researchers followed their own interests and do not claim that the result is representative of Coventry women during this period. Their articles merely scratch the surface, for there are many incredible stories still untold. They hope to inspire others to continue to look into the fascinating history of Coventry women who have done so much to fashion the city and the lives of its people.

ACKNOWLEDGEMENTS

The Group would like to thank the following organisations and individuals for their help in preparing this book:

Local Studies, Central Library, Coventry for research and permission to reproduce the photograph of Winifred Barrow.

Coventry Records Office for research and permission to use the photograph of Beryl Aylward.

The Coventry Evening Telegraph for allowing us to use the photograph of Margaret Rylatt.

Individuals who have supplied information and photographs of themselves or relatives.

CONTENTS

INTRODUCTION iii
ACKNOWLEDGEMENTS iii
1. BERYL AYLWARD 1
2. WINIFRED MERRICK BARROW 8
3. GERTRUDE BILLSON 11
4. ANGELA BRAZIL 15
5. NELLIE CARTER 20
6. SHEILA COLLINS 21
7. JOAN DAVISON 26
8. SELINA DIX 35
9. KATHLEEN DIXON 39
10. CATHERINE GRAY 45
11. MURIEL GRIMMETT-OFFLEY 47
12. ANTONIA HOCKTON 48
13. BARBARA LEA 50
14. S. W. MICHELL 54
15. MARY MONTES 58
16. PEGGY RICHARDS 61
17. FLO ROBINSON 64
18 MARGARET RYLATT 71
19. JESSIE SADLER 77
20. KAY NEWSON (formerly SWEENEY) 81

Beryl Aylward.

In the summer of 1932 a huge controversy hit the headlines, when a young Coventry teacher refused to take part in the Empire Day celebrations that year. Her actions were not taken lightly, but as a Quaker and a pacifist she objected strongly to the militaristic manifestations that the celebrations upheld.

Born in Coventry on 22nd May 1906, Beryl was educated first of all at Centaur Road School, Earlsdon until the age of ten and continued at two Quaker boarding schools, Sibford and Ackworth. She acquired a degree in English at Birmingham University and attended Woodbrooke Teacher Training College for her qualification to teach. Here she lived in a very cosmopolitan atmosphere with students who came from many countries to the Quaker International College. The ethos of the college was that of pacifism, internationalism and goodwill to others. It was unusual at that time for a primary school teacher to have a degree as well as a teaching certificate. By 1932, when she was twenty-six years old, she had been teaching for four years.

When Beryl learned of the plans to celebrate Empire Day on 24th May 1932 at Red Lane School, her conscience would not allow her to take part. The previous year she had done so, however unwillingly, but in 1932 something about the overt militarism of the programme forced her into an action that was to have profound consequences. First of all she spoke to the headmistress, Miss H. Croft, asking to be excused from taking part in the activities. She did not want to absent herself from school and would see that her charges were left in the care of another teacher, but would then go to her classroom and mark books. The headmistress responded by saying that she need not take any active role, sing songs, etc., but her presence was required. Beryl believed that this was just as bad, that by being present she was silently condoning the sentiments of the occasion. The headmistress said she would have to write to the Director of Education, Frank Harrod, if she wanted to take it further.

She sent her letter on 11th May 1932 asking for leave to absent herself from the celebrations on conscientious grounds. His reply came promptly that permission was denied. He justified his stand by saying that the Education Committee had decreed that all schools under its jurisdiction should take part in Empire Day celebrations.

'Obviously, as a servant of that committee, you have no option but to obey such instructions and attend the celebrations at the school at which you are employed.' [1]

On the 23rd May he sent another letter to Beryl reiterating his first, stating that she was expected to remain in charge of her class and carry out her duties. This suggests that Beryl had written again in the hope of softening his attitude. This did not happen.

As the Empire Day celebrations took place at Red Lane School, Beryl did exactly as she had said she would, taking her pupils into the hall and leaving them in the charge of others while she marked books in her classroom. As a consequence of her actions the Director of Education sent her a letter, dated 25th May, stating that the committee had considered her actions and decided.
1. To suspend you immediately from your duties at the school.
2. To recommend the E.C. to terminate your engagement immediately. [2]
Following this curt note, another letter was despatched to Beryl on 28th May requesting her presence at an interview with the Primary and Post Primary Schools' sub-committee with reference to her suspension. This was to take place on Monday 30th May at 4.15pm. In her diary she listed the questions that were put to her at that interview:
1. How is it that you are the only one to object out of 600 teachers?
2. Hasn't your religion taught you to do your duty and obey those in authority over you?
3. Don't you respect St. Paul's saying 'Fear God and honour thy King.'
4. Do you believe in the abolition of slavery?
5. How would you take an Empire Day celebration?
6. Have you any conscientious objection against taking your cheque as you seem to have this objection against carrying out our instructions?
7. Do you intend to apologise to this committee and to the headmistress of your school?
8. Would you take the same action again? [3]

There were some strange questions amongst them, but they seemed to be trying to combat her objections with religious arguments. How did they know that there were no others objectors? There may have been others who just did not have the courage to stand up publicly like her. We do not know what she said in reply, but she must have argued her case and stood by her principles, as there was no easing of the attitude of the committee. There followed a meeting of the Education Committee in camera to discuss the case, leading to another letter to Beryl on 6th June confirming her dismissal. Many Labour councillors took up her cause such as Sidney Stringer and George Hodgkinson, but in some ways their response turned the whole episode into a political issue. The NUT disassociated itself from the case on the grounds that she was not a member of the union, although she had letters of support from individual members.

Throughout June and July of 1932 the controversy filled the columns of the local and national press. Following the report on 7th June in the Midland Daily Telegraph relating to the closed meeting, Beryl wrote to the paper to put her case, as she believed that their report had given an incorrect impression. Other local newspapers took up the story including the Coventry Herald, the Coventry Standard and the Birmingham Gazette, whose correspondent actually secured an interview with Beryl. She remained true to her convictions, reiterating her objection to the militaristic tone of the celebrations, with its undue stress on national power and prestige. As a Quaker and a pacifist it was unacceptable to her on conscientious grounds. Letters of support as well as a few against Beryl began appearing in the newspapers from 13th June.

Richard Lee, set the tone on 15th June in the Midland Daily Telegraph, stating that the wisest men of all parties were supporting Beryl's cause. That it was unfair of civil authorities to coerce its servants to be false to their religion. An ambiguous letter was printed in the same newspaper from Mary Dormer Harris, seemingly against Beryl's actions on the grounds that duty should come first, but went on to say that disarmament was in the air and she believed that we were not a war loving people. She obviously had some criticism of her letter for she wrote a personal one of support to Beryl. Others used this issue as a platform to put forward their own particular theories. One such was Mrs. F. Stokes whose letter was also printed in the Midland Daily Telegraph on 15th June. She wrote on behalf of the 'Workers, Anti-war Movement' complaining of the high-handedness of the local authority. She said that the Education Committee was trying to foster the 'war mind' among children. She went on to say that the children of Coventry are 'dragooned into the playground and forced, even against their wishes and that of their parents, to pay homage to an Empire built on the bodies of teeming millions of slaves and only held now by ruthless use of armed forces...' Included in her many complaints she condemned the Scout Movement and the Boys Brigade. This initiated another crop of letters from local leaders of those two organisations defending their record on peaceable aims and activities. All the while deviating from the issue of Beryl's dismissal.

Even the church was not free of this aspect when a letter of support was sent to the Midland Daily Telegraph, which appeared on 20th June 1932, on behalf of The Coventry Fellowship of Clergy and Ministers. It also advocated freedom of religious conscience and was signed by Norman L. Robinson and H. Ingli James. Two days later a response was printed from Canon Morton disassociating himself from the decision of the Fellowship, saying that it was just a personal opinion of the two signatories. Back came a letter from the two original correspondents justifying themselves, which reflected very badly on Canon Morton. The majority of churchmen gave support to Beryl's cause, some even organised a demonstration in the Market Square in Coventry.

Of the many letters that appeared in print the majority were defending Beryl and against the Education Committee for their dictatorial manner. Many pressed for reinstatement and support groups were formed to highlight her situation. The story was taken up by the national press and articles appeared in The Daily Herald, The Manchester Guardian, The News Chronicle and Reynolds as well as the Society of Friends' own newspaper, The Friend. All the publicity stimulated many people to write to Beryl, not just from the local area, but countrywide. An interesting letter, dated 10th June, came from Mrs. G. Jacobs of Coventry, who agreed entirely with Beryl's sentiments and was also a teacher, who felt indignant at the injustice Beryl had suffered. She asserted that in her school there was no problem, as each teacher was allowed individual choice of how to celebrate Empire Day in her own classroom. This woman's communication refutes the Education Committee's allegation that no other teacher in Coventry had objected.

Another letter, also dated 10th June, came from Gwladus M. Cudbird of Gabalfa, Cardiff. She had read about the case in the newspaper and wrote a letter of support. She too had made a stand against the 'unquakerly ritual' as she called it, but had received only understanding from her headmaster and the rest of the staff. Wales did not celebrate the occasion, she claimed, in the same manner as in England. Her husband had been imprisoned in the First World War as a conscientious objector, so she understood what it was to stand up for your principles.

An unusual letter of support was sent to Beryl on 12th June from a young man who signed himself Edward. He applauded her moral courage and called her 'a noble woman.' He wished his own teachers had possessed her convictions, instead of shifting their own consciences to conform. As an atheist, he believed that she might not take his letter seriously and would wish to burn it, but it is unlikely that Beryl would have thought any the less of him for having his own beliefs and the proof of that is the fact that she kept his letter with the others for the rest of her life.

Many correspondents offered to help her get another job in their area if she wished. Others asked her to attend meetings and seminars. Those that were teachers told her of their own strategy to circumvent the question of celebrating Empire Day in the traditional manner, by talking to their pupils about the movement for peace, the work of the League of Nations, or as one shorthand teacher did dictated peace addresses to her students. There was even a letter from a Frenchwoman, Marie Bachmann, who had heard of her case in the press and was moved to write a letter of sympathy and support. She encouraged Beryl to take up Esperanto, as she had found it so interesting and through it had made many friends. She obviously passed on Beryl's name to her correspondents, as numerous letters and postcards in that language arrived at Beryl's home from all parts of Europe. A notable personality like Bertrand Russell, whose pacifist views were well known, was driven to write a letter in support of Beryl, published in the Birmingham Gazette on 25th June. It became such a burning issue that questions were asked in Parliament.

It is interesting to see how the envelopes were addressed to Beryl. She must have been very well known to the Post Office at the time. Some went to Red Lane

School and some to the Education Department, which had to be redirected. That must have been very galling for her headmistress and the council officers who had brought about her dismissal. One was addressed to:
   Miss Aylward,
   Quaker,
      One-time Elementary Assistant School Mistress,
      Coventry.
Another was addressed to:
   Miss Beryl Aylward,
   Ex-School Teacher for Conscience Sake,
   Coventry,
      Warwicks.
A few were addressed to the Friends Meeting House, as they knew that they would be passed on safely. All correspondents seemed supremely confident that their letters would arrive and it would be comforting to think that they all did. More than fifty letters reached Beryl in the few months subsequent to her dismissal.

Reports of the Council meeting concerned with Beryl's reinstatement came out at the end of June 1932. The Midland Daily Telegraph of 28th June reported that a protester had been forcibly removed from the public gallery. A resolution was passed by twenty-seven to twenty-five votes to reinvestigate Beryl's case. They went over the old ground stating that the original plans, which had been acceptable to Beryl, were changed by the headmistress and she felt unable to take part. It suggests a clash of personalities between the headmistress and her young teacher. The Coventry Herald of 1st July gave a fuller account of the proceedings in council. The Bishop of Birmingham had obviously publicly defended Beryl and the Mayor, Alderman Vincent Wyles, responded rather testily that the Bishop should mind his own business and not interfere.

The council tried to justify its actions by declaring that she was deliberately disobedient and defiant at her interview. The Mayor said that she had shown extreme bitterness towards the British Empire. Councillor Stringer accused the Mayor of bias. She was accused of neglecting her duty by absenting herself from the occasion. Councillor Payne suggested that there was a political motive to Beryl's actions. Councillor Rose obviously believed that the debate was getting out of hand when he asked if they were going to 'crucify Miss Aylward on a cross of Imperialism.' Councillor Flinn seemed to be the only moderating voice in the council chamber. He remarked that far from being defiant he had found her 'a quiet little mouse.' He felt that the letters to the newspapers had done her cause no good at all. If the headmistress had handled the situation better, nothing more would have been heard of it.

The Midland Daily Telegraph reported on 26th July that the Council had voted by thirty-four votes to twenty not to reinstate Beryl and upheld the decision of the

Education Committee to dismiss her. In the end the Council did not want to lose face by climbing down from their entrenched position. In taking their decision they were fully aware that it would be impossible for her to get another job in the city and might prejudice her chances in the future.

The Society of Friends set up a special support committee to help Beryl in any way that they could. First of all they enquired into the circumstances of her dismissal. Her views were in line with Quaker beliefs and not due to any political motive. An interview was arranged for Beryl in London, with the Central Education Committee of the Society of Friends, where she explained the circumstances of her case. They corresponded with Coventry Education Committee, but that body was adamant in its decision. The Friends committee tried to help her obtain another teaching post by putting out the word and the results were passed on to Beryl for her to take further. The committee met five times between June and September 1932, but it only disbanded in February 1933 when she obtained a post at Lutterworth Central School.

Even then the controversy did not die down. Beryl received a letter, dated 12th April 1933, from W. Hope Jones of Eton College, who was a member of the Ypres League, a pacifist organisation, telling her of an extremely reactionary article against disarmament in the Ypres Times. The article was written by Admiral W.E. R. Martin and stated that a communist teacher had refused to take the children out flag flying on Empire Day. It referred to Beryl, but the writer had turned her from a pacifist into a communist for his own propaganda. Mr. Hope Jones, incensed by the article, asked her permission to write back and put the record straight. She replied and he sent her a copy of his letter (although this is not in the Records Office).

Beryl began a new life when she left Coventry for Lutterworth in 1933, and must have tried to put the events of the previous year behind her. During the early part of the war she was working in Sutton, Surrey. While there she received many letters from her mother keeping her abreast of events in Coventry. Beryl's mother shared her daughter's sentiments about pacifism and was horrified at the developments of the war and the devastation it caused. Following the November blitz of 1940, Mrs. Aylward wrote to tell her daughter that they were safe, but like many they were without gas or electricity, although they had some water. The windows were smashed, but they did not appear to have any structural damage to their bungalow in Bates Road. In her description of the damage to the city she calls Coventry 'a city of the dead.'

Beryl spent eight years as the headmistress of Halesowen School for Girls, where she became involved in local politics. Her interest was sufficient to induce her to stand as a candidate for the Central Ward of the Borough of Halesowen in November 1945. Her final post before returning to Coventry, was as a lecturer at Newton Training College, Bath.

In 1956 Beryl was appointed as headmistress of Templars Secondary Modern School for Girls. The old controversy was not fully forgotten, as it was mentioned in the report of her appointment in the Coventry Evening Telegraph of 30th November 1956. However, she did not dwell on the events of 1932 and many of her teachers were unaware of the controversy. A young teacher who worked under her headship in 1964 was totally ignorant of her dispute with the Education Authority so many years before. Beryl concentrated her energy into guiding the pupils through their school years and into the world of work. She initiated a scheme of work experience, approaching local factories, offices and shops to take her final year girls for a week or two. This became standard practice in many schools in future years.

Another of her innovations was the exchange of senior pupils with girls from other schools in different parts of the country. Girls were allowed time away from lessons to entertain their guests, by taking them to places of interest in the city and the surrounding area. The object of these exchanges was to teach girls to widen their horizons. They had to learn to live in harmony with their visitors, both at home and on outings. It was an exercise in understanding others, as much as a pleasant relief from lessons. Return visits could be made to rural areas totally different from city living, creating a comprehensive view of other people's lives.

When Beryl retired in 1967 she moved from Coventry to Oadby, in Leicestershire, to be near to her brother, Bernard. She continued to live in Leicestershire until her death in 1984. She was a woman who lived by her religious convictions without compromise. She was not afraid to take on the city council when she believed she was right, but did it in a quietly determined way.

Footnotes
1. Coventry Records Office, access number 1025/1/1.
2. Ibid. 1025/1/3.
3. Ibid. 1025/38/1/1.

Sources
Coventry Records Office. Access numbers:
1025   Correspondence re. Dismissal.
1035   Records 1918-65.
1036   Notice of candidature in 1945 election in Halesowen.
1045   Family papers 1878-1926.
Book of newspaper cuttings, Reserved Collection, Local Studies, Central Library, Coventry.

Acknowledgements.
Thank you to Eileen Castle for suggesting Beryl Aylward as a suitable subject for this book.

Winifred Merrick Barrow
1892-1957

Winifred Merrick Barrow was born in Cheshire, the daughter of a vicar, in the year 1892.

Liverpool appears to be the city where she received her formal education. She attended Melrose High School and Liverpool University. She held a Master of Arts degree and also the Diploma of Social Science. Her first few years as a teacher, from 1913 to 1926, were spent in Liverpool schools. And, as well as teaching, she found time to be the secretary of the North Office of the Personal Service Committee at the Victoria Settlement, Liverpool. In 1926 she left her home town and took up the post of senior history mistress at the City of Worcester Secondary Grammar School, and it was here that she spent the next six years of her life.

When Barr's Hill School opened in 1908, Miss Grace Howell was appointed as the first headmistress and for 24 years she developed the school and cared for the education of the girls. Upon her retirement in 1932 a successor was appointed and so Winifred Merrick Barrow came to Coventry.

She was one of that dedicated band of spinster ladies who chose to forego the rewards of a family of their own but regarded their pupils as their "children" and brought to their school the feeling of family life. One of her guiding principles was that a school should be a place halfway between home and the outside world. It should be large enough to be a community but small enough for its girls to be treated as individuals.

And so began an era of 21 years during which time the outside world, and Coventry itself, were to change beyond all recognition.

Miss Barrow's first years were described by her second mistress, Miss Scholes, as "happy years when we seemed to extend and improve our school activities every year." One of her main problems being the increasing school roll and finding sufficient accommodation for them all. However, this was to pale into insignificance when, in 1939, war on Germany was declared.

Miss Barrow seems to have worked closely with Miss Michell, the headmistress of Stoke Park Girls School, during these trying times. Some girls from both schools were immediately evacuated to Leamington where they were thought to be safe. Here they joined with Leamington High School. At this time the war was in its very early stages and as nothing appeared to be happening these girls soon returned to Coventry. But, on November 14th 1940, Coventry was brought terrifyingly to the forefront of war itself and again some girls from both Barr's Hill and Stoke Park were evacuated, but this time to Atherstone. It was Miss Barrow who went with them. Like many others in Coventry her home was to suffer damage from incendiary bombs. But, again, Miss Scholes records that throughout the war Miss Barrow's "cheerful sympathy never faltered ----."

After the war the continuing problem of insufficient accommodation still had to be resolved. For not only were more girls attending the school, the school itself had suffered war damage and this took time to repair. However, with her usual calm and fortitude Miss Barrow met and addressed each new problem as it arose.

As well as her strong commitment to the school, Miss Barrow gave much to the local community. For two years she was a teachers' representative to the Local Education Authority. As a member of the Coventry Head Teachers' Association she was their president from 1948-49. Also from 1945-50 she was a member of the Coventry City Guild. Her interests spread beyond Coventry with membership of the Joint Council of Midland Headmistresses and Hospital Matrons, and membership, also, of the National Council of Women.

For three years, prior to her retirement, she served as a magistrate. Amongst the many tributes paid to her on her last appearance on the Bench, it was said "Miss Barrow had graced the Bench and was held in the highest possible respect."

In July 1953, Miss Barrow retired from Barr's Hill School. Upon her departure she said "----- I cannot pretend that I shall not have any backward thoughts. Coventry has been very kind to me. The difficulties through which the school has passed have welded us into a happy united group, and I have been enriched by my experience here." On leaving Coventry, Miss Barrow returned to her Northern roots to live with her brother who was Vicar in the Lancashire moorland village of Belmont. Sadly, her brother was to die in 1956.

Miss Barrow, herself, died on February 11th 1957 in a hospital near Liverpool where she had been ill for several weeks.

Winifred Merrick Barrow was a gracious lady who worked tirelessly for others with gentleness and with serenity. Her deeply-rooted religious faith had sustained her throughout her life. Whilst in Coventry she had gained a reputation for quiet unassuming efficiency and was highly respected by all who knew her.

Personal Footnote: When autumn comes and the leaves drop from the trees it inevitably falls to someone to clear them up. The grounds of Barr's Hill were beautiful and part of this beauty was the lovely old trees. As well as being dotted round the gardens they also surrounded the playing fields and one dinner-time, three young pupils in their first term at this esteemed school came upon these piles of leaves which the caretaker had painstakingly swept up. With no thought they spent a wonderful half hour jumping in and out of these lovely, rustly, beautiful piles of leaves. Exhilarated, they returned to their afternoon classes. The lessons had hardly begun when a message came to the room --- Would the girls who had disturbed the piles of leaves in the grounds please report to the headmistress's room. With great embarrassment the three girls concerned presented themselves outside the Barrow's study. She did not shout or rave but gently pointed out how thoughtless they had been after all the caretaker's hard work. It was then suggested that they repair the damage they had caused by sweeping up the leaves into piles again. So the three reprobates spent the next hour gathering together all the leaves which they had so recently disturbed. A lesson learnt but delivered in a gentle and knowing way.

However, even after all these years, I still can't resist a pile of lovely autumn leaves!

Sources.
Midland Daily Telegraph/Coventry Evening Telegraph.
Barr's Hill School Magazines. Local Studies, Central Library, Coventry.

Gertrude Billson.

The following extracts and information are taken from 'As I Remember,' by Jillian Vernon, who wanted to record her years growing up in a happy family, to pass on her memories to the next generation. Her father, Thomas, was in the building trade and her mother, Gertrude, looked after the home and eventually five children. However, it is the enterprise and determination of her mother, which illuminates the story. Had she been born in a more modern era, she would have been a career businesswoman, but frustrated by the conventions of pre-war Britain, she channelled her energy into domestic projects to the benefit of her family.

Gertrude and Thomas Billson were married in 1932, in the village of Arley, just outside Coventry. Three children, Peter, Janet and Jillian, were born over the following five years. They lived in several villages near Arley, before moving to Middlemarch Road in Coventry. Too poor to afford a holiday, Gertrude acquired a tent through a credit club, at one shilling in the pound. This enabled the family to take their first holiday to the south coast in 1937. Their only means of transport was a motorbike and sidecar, already altered to accommodate their growing family and nicknamed "The Blackberry Basket." To this was added a trailer for the camping equipment, made from a tea chest, costing sixpence and the wheels of Gertrude's bicycle.

During the winter, Mom bought some canvas and extended the tent, both in length and height. Dad bought some plywood to put over the camp bed so that during the day it could be used as a table.

During the war, the bombing of Coventry forced the family out of their rented home in Radford, which backed onto the grounds of the Daimler factory. Gertrude and the children went to live in Arley with relatives, while Thomas was away in the Air Force. He would send parcels of sweets and goodies to the children, whenever he could and managed to get home on leave as often as possible. A new baby boy, called Tony, was born to Gertrude while she was evacuated at Arley. The family returned to Coventry in 1942 and rented a house in Victory Road. Short of money, Gertrude began to make dolls to sell to her neighbours and their friends.

......using her precious clothing coupons, she bought material to make dresses and bonnets for the dolls. She bought more crock heads and raided our pillows and pillowcases to make the bodies. The sewing machine was red hot and Mom was kept busy with yet more orders coming in. She worked late at night, but her one problem was finding material for the dresses and bonnets, as she was

running out of clothing coupons. She then had the brilliant idea of making toy elephants out of redundant air force blankets.

When Thomas was home on leave he too joined in the enterprise. His contribution was trains and trucks made from wood and dried milk tins. Another boy, Colin, was born towards the end of the war. Although they were unable to get away for holidays at the seaside, Gertrude was determined to take the children away for breaks in the summer, despite the difficulties. She extended the tent once again to accommodate the two youngest children and set off with all five children to a camp site at Meriden. It was when she saw the caravans on the site, that she first had the idea of building one for themselves. When the war came to an end and Thomas returned to civilian life, she set about turning her ideas into reality.

She saw an advert in the paper for a lorry chassis and talked Dad into going to see it. The outcome was that they built their first caravan in our back garden. Mom worked on it just as much as Dad; we children were allowed to do a bit of painting towards the end, but at that time, with Mom busy working on the caravan, we had to do more jobs around the house....

As they lived in a mid-terraced house with no back entrance, they had to solve the problem of getting the finished caravan, called "The Muddlins," on to the road. A hired lorry was driven across the recreation ground to the rear of the property, the fence was removed, the caravan was hoisted on to the lorry and the fence re-erected. The caravan was transported to a site in Weymouth, where it remained for many years.

In 1946 the family moved from Coventry to Small Heath, Birmingham, where Thomas set up his own building business. The house was spacious, but needed a substantial amount of renovation work to bring it up to standard. It was the first home that the Billson's had owned and this gave Gertrude greater impetus to carry out her home improvement ideas. She did not like the L-shaped living-room and was adamant that a more useful space could be created by removing the kitchen wall.

Dad realised that if he didn't make a start on the alterations, then Mom would do it when he was at work. Mom admitted that she didn't like housework, she would much sooner have a hammer in her hand than a duster. We had to admit that Mom's idea was a great improvement. We now could have the table in the centre of the room and still have room to play around.

Not content with her achievement in the kitchen/dining-room Gertrude turned her attention to another source of discontent with the house, namely the staircase. She thought the hall would be much improved if the staircase was turned around.

Knowing that Dad would find some objection, she took a couple of floorboards up to see which way the joists were running; she could see no problem so, after giving Dad his tea, she put the suggestion to him. "Can't be done" said Dad, "Yes it can " says Mom, "I have checked, and if you do it this way it will be fine." Needless to say, the stairs were turned around and it made a very large hallway.

Needing more space as the family grew up, Gertrude decided that a loft conversion would solve the problem. This project was completed without argument from Thomas and some help from their two prospective sons-in-law, who learned all the basics of DIY from Gertrude.

Following the success of their first self-built caravan, they decided to make others. "The Beehive" came next, followed by "The Silver Lining," all transported to Weymouth to join "The Muddlins." When not in use by the family, they were let to holiday makers. Not content with this Gertrude had another idea.

Mom then became really ambitious and thought "Why not make a caravan which would fold down." So with the aid of two shoe boxes, she explained to Dad what she had in mind. Once again Dad thought she was mad, but decided it best to humour her and to his surprise it worked. That caravan was given the name "The Low Cot." We often wonder if perhaps, that was the forerunner of all fold down caravans.

They now had a mobile caravan, but no car with which to tow it. A solution was found when they exchanged "The Beehive" for a Standard Flying 12 car, which they christened "Jane."

Mom wasn't satisfied with what they had already made, she wanted to make a caravan which would fold even smaller. That was when "The Stow-away" was born. By now they had exchanged "Jane" for a Standard Vanguard which was called "Moggie."

When daughters, Janet and Jillian, married in the mid 1950's, their mother helped to rearrange the house, which her daughters initially shared, by turning it into two flats.

While we were talking downstairs, Mom was busy upstairs all at once there was banging going on, and the next we knew Mom was taking out a fireplace from one of the bedrooms.

Once this project was complete Gertrude decided that their own house was too big now that the two girls had left home. They settled on a pair of cottages in the village of Over Whitacre, which the vendors would not sell separately. However, Gertrude and Thomas could only afford one of the pair and the one they liked best had sitting tenants. Undaunted, they persuaded the sitting tenants to buy the other semi, on the understanding that the Billsons would install a bathroom. This arrangement accomplished, they were able to move into the house they desired.

Once Mom and Dad moved in, the house didn't know what had hit it. They built an extension on the side of the house which gave a bathroom upstairs and kitchen downstairs. They had to replace the floor in one of the downstairs rooms as there had previously been very bad flooding which had done quite a lot of damage.

They liked the countryside, but they began to feel rather isolated. As both of their daughters now lived in Coventry, with their families, they decided to move to the city themselves in 1962. They chose a house in Fir Tree Avenue, Tile Hill, which suited their needs and required just a little attention.

Once the garden was clear, work started on the house. The bathroom at that time was at the front of the house, but Mom didn't like that, so it was moved to the back. The kitchen was completely restyled, and there was a silly little veranda at the back which had to come down.

Once the work was complete they all had a holiday, grandparents, their children and grandchildren, in North Wales. It was so successful, they all decided to do the same the following year. However, as they were preparing for the holiday Gertrude became ill and went into hospital for tests, which delayed their arrival in Wales. Following her return Gertrude was diagnosed with a tumour on the brain and went into hospital for surgery to remove the growth. The operation left her paralysed on the left side and confined to a wheelchair for the last eleven years of her life. Unable to move without assistance, Thomas fitted a pulley chain above her bed, to allow her to sit upright when she wished. No longer able to fulfil an active role in the house, she took to filling out the football pools in the hope of winning a fortune, not to benefit herself, but for her family who gave her such devoted care.

Acknowledgements.
Many thanks to Jillian Vernon and Janet Baker for allowing the use of extracts from 'As I Remember' to be used in this profile.

ANGELA BRAZIL

Angela Brazil was a product of her class and age, at a time when the social structure of the country was more defined than now. Her experiences, therefore, were limited to the code and conduct of the middle classes in which she was brought up. But personality too helped to shape and produce the strong willed and rather determined character who arrived in Coventry at the age of forty-two, already well established as an author of many 'schoolgirl' novels.

She was born at Preston in 1869, the second daughter, and youngest child of Angelica and Clarence Brazil. Her mother, half Scottish and half Spanish, came from a family of shipping line owners, her father of Irish descent was the manager of a cotton mill. The young Brazils, elder brothers Clarence and Walter and sister Amy, together with their sister Angela, lived a comfortable and, it would seem, a charmed life in the pleasant suburbs around the north west of England. There may have been financial difficulties, but her autobiography makes it clear that she was unaware of them. The house at Westcliffe Terrace in Preston was to be the first of many homes Angela would experience. When she was five the family moved to Egremont, on the Cheshire side of the Mersey. Three and a half years later came the move to Greenhayes in Manchester followed by another move to Rusholme, also in Manchester, before the move to Belmont, at the edge of Bolton Moors. And finally, in adult life, to Coventry.

None of the moves or the frequent changes of school appear to have distressed her greatly, although she was upset at leaving the countryside around Egremont for urban Manchester. Some of the moves, it appears, were specifically made to bring her into the area of a better school. Her mother appeared to take control of the schooling; her father quite happy to provide for the family without imposing his will. He was a strict churchgoer who tried to enlighten his children and not suppress them.

Although private education was a standard for the Brazils, Angela's experiences would suggest that standards in quality, teaching methods and range of subjects differed widely.

Her first school, The Turrets, concentrated on book learning. There she read, remembered and repeated facts. Dull though this must have been there does not seem to have been much rebellion, except about maths. It all seemed to have been compensated for by her affection for the younger children, whom she was quite happy to 'mother', a trait followed through into adult life. And, of course, friendships. Those schoolgirl friendships which she never tired of forming. Perhaps, in part, to make up for the blow she had received from her relationship eagerly formed with Effie, a pupil at The Turrets. After waiting excitedly for the school holidays and Effie's expected three week visit, she was cruelly disappointed to find Effie would only be coming for one week, the other two to be spent with a new friend. Effie's candid remark to Angela during her visit that she hadn't wanted to come, but liked it now that she was there, must have been a shattering experience.

Whatever else the school might give her daughter, Angelica made sure it taught her the correct modes and manners of her place in society. The Preparatory High School in Manchester had not come up to expectations. Angela had acquired rather slipshod habits such as skipping home, sliding on the pavements and running into shops to buy sweets. Friends had not been invited home. Education and refinement were finally found at the Ellerslie School in Manchester. It was also the happiest school for Angela and she seems to have flourished there.

Despite the hard work and successful exam results, university did not seem to have been suggested by her mother or father, and Angela found the cramming for the Higher Cambridge Certificate hard and stressful. Academic life did not appeal to her. The boys needed a career and, therefore, a university education but, in all probability, Angelica would not have seen working for a living as a suitable occupation for Angela.

It was not all school though. When Angela was fourteen the family acquired a cottage in Llanbedr in North Wales. This was a place she immediately fell in love with. To her it was freedom. It was also unusual for a family of her class to spend their holidays in such surroundings. The cottage was small and primitive but after the constraints of urban Manchester this was wild and exciting. Even the journey there was adventurous with the final stage by ferry across the River Conway, sometimes in the company of sheep or a horse and cart.

This wild out of the way place, however, was to be central in helping to establish her as a successful writer. But in the year after she left school, art seemed to have been her chosen path. Amy had already completed a year at art school in Manchester and followed this by a period at Heatherley's in London. Angela decided to join her there. Wild country she may have loved, but London also caught her imagination and she threw herself into London cultural life with visits to most of the museums and galleries in company with a circle of friends.

Life after London seems to have continued with the minimum of trouble. Angela and Amy continued to paint for themselves, visiting places as far afield as the Lake District and Weobley in Herefordshire.

At Llanbedr she indulged her other talent, creating stories. The Welsh countryside with its associations of magic and superstition was a rich breeding ground for her imagination. Not modest with her talents, she began to entertain the younger children in the district with her stories, particularly on wet days. Her audience, curled up among the hay in the barn, with the rain beating on the roof, were captive and enthralled.

Life in the town saw some changes. By 1898 Clarence had moved away and was practising as a solicitor in Lancaster. The family house had been sold and Mr and Mrs Brazil with Amy moved to a house in Bangor Street, Bolton. Angela on returning from London had gone to keep house for Walter at Bolton Le Moors, an arrangement which was to continue for the rest of her life. Whether marriage was hoped for is not known. The family seem to have been close and self-sufficient and not until her 30th birthday did Angela have to cope with any major changes.

In 1899 her father, Clarence, died leaving the three women alone. With no reason to be at home all the time the three now travelled abroad frequently. Not only did they visit the more familiar tourist haunts of Venice, Rome and Pompeii but Egypt and Nazareth too.

Angela's stories too had been transposed to paper. In the same year as her father died her first book was published 'The Mischievous Brownie'. This was a volume of four children's plays with a fairytale element. Her storytelling had prompted her family to encourage her to write down her stories and when the family sold the cottage in Llanbedr and bought a larger farmhouse in the same village, Angela claimed the garden studio for her study. Her first novel 'A Terrible Tomboy' was published in 1904 and was well received, although it was not the genre she was later to become famous for. The schoolgirl books began with 'The Fortunes of Philippa' based on her mother's unhappy experiences in an English boarding school, after her less rigid and controlled life in Rio de Janeiro. This was probably Angela's best attempt at portraying the psychology of her heroine. Blackie & Son were pleased to accept it and many more of her novels in the future. Her books sold for almost three quarters of a century and earned Angela a very good income. Ironically, Angela herself had only been a boarder for the last term at Ellerslie. There she seemed to have thrown herself into boarding school life with midnight feasts, secret societies and friendships. Her mother's unhappy experiences did not seem to have worried her and one of her prejudices that remained with her was that day girls were inferior to boarders.

In 1911 Walter bought the successful practice of Doctor Milner-Moore in Coventry and moved into 1 The Quadrant, the most exclusive residential area in the city. Angela stayed with him as housekeeper and Amy, now a practising nurse, took up a post in Stratford Hospital and lived near there with her mother. In 1915 Angelica died and Amy moved to Coventry to be with Angela and Walter.

Angela was still writing and travelling, but with her usual energy involved herself wholly in the social life of Coventry's elite. Soon after they arrived both Walter and herself joined the Coventry Natural History and Scientific Society. There she pursued many of the activities offered. She did a series of watercolour sketches, gave talks and went on many rambles. Evenings often ended at the Geisha Café in Hertford Street. In summer the rambles were weekly and among those most notable were the rambles in the Brownshill Green woodlands, now covered with housing. Other rambles included a train ride to Kenilworth and tea in an old timbered cottage at Ashow.

She quickly made herself known at the local girls schools where she seems to have been welcomed. The Quadrant High School, Cheshunt School and Queens Road School were all schools where she was known and involved. This involvement with young girls seems to have continued into the social life at 1 The Quadrant. Angela was always giving children's parties. The Quadrant house was suitably large enough and well staffed to make these events memorable for the children. Rooms to change in, rooms to leave outdoor shoes in and, of course, a room to eat in. Jellies and cakes, table-creams, biscuits and buns were all served by Amy and Angela and the two maids. What was not allowed was the crossing over of the social classes. The orphanage children who attended a specially prepared party for them would on no occasion be allowed to meet the other children who frequented the house for their parties.

In May 1914 some members of the Coventry Natural History and Scientific Society felt that there was a need to form another society to preserve the antiquities of Coventry. Angela again was in the forefront, although there were hints of rivalry between herself and Miss Dormer Harris. But it was at Angela's house that the sub-committee met to discuss the formation of a museum. By 1918 the City Guild, as they became known, acquired the crypt of St. Mary's for their museum. The Brazils, collectors themselves, donated gloves worn by George Eliot, mouldings and carvings and some dolls.

Wartime found Angela helping in a creche, allowing women to work in the munitions factories. At the beginning of the war she was elected onto the committee of the YWCA and later became its president. A local newspaper in 1938 gave a report in its social column of an evening presided over by Angela, in which she gave a speech in the form of a news bulletin. The atmosphere of a girls' school party remained, with references to Miss Carter having won the cookery championship and the announcement that the girls' Country Cottage at Corley, which Angela was donating for the use of the YWCA, would shortly open with a house-warming party. It is interesting that at that time the same paper reported on the need for a hostel for working girls, the YWCA being too expensive for them. The inaugural weekend at Corley Moor was well publicised with a photograph of Angela and the Committee outside the cottage. The report of the weekend could have come straight from one of her books. 'Five of the members spent the weekend in the cottage and, from all accounts, a jolly good weekend it was too!'

This busy social life which remained until 1939 included events outside Coventry. Angela had bought herself a house at Polperro in Cornwall and spent a lot of her time there. Again, she seems to have had no trouble involving herself in the community there and with its elite. It seemed she had several meetings with Sir Hugh Walpole, Sir Arthur Quiller-Couch and Dr Marie Stopes. Apparently, Angela was the first to make the overture to Dr Stopes and when the two women met they found they liked one another. Angela, however, refused Dr Stopes's request to adapt one of her school stories for the stage, modestly writing to her that '...I don't believe there is a single one of the books that you could use for the purpose with any chance of success.'

Despite writing her novels she did not neglect her artistic pursuits and with Amy gave an exhibition at the Walker Gallery in New Bond Street. She also broadcast and gave talks at Harrods in London. In Coventry she extended her activities to cathedral committee work and watched the museum grow until, in 1930, it was taken over by Coventry Corporation.

Her generosity and time given to these many activities makes it difficult to understand her attitude to her brother Clarence's marriage. Clarence, the only one of the family living apart, had met and married a woman twenty years his junior. Worse than that, the sister of a piano manufacturer. The family at The Quadrant was outraged and their treatment of Florence, his wife, was mean spirited and hurtful. Unacknowledged, she was never welcomed at the house. Her only compensation was that in later life she inherited the house and contents from Amy, probably as payment for her services as Amy's carer.

Angela continued to write and in August 1946 Blackie & Son published 'The School on the Loch', the background for the book taken from a holiday spent in Scotland near her publisher, Mr Walter Blackie. It was her last completed novel. On 11 March 1947 after having supper with Walter and Amy she went to bed in a good mood. In the morning, however, they found her dead. Within four months Walter was dead and in 1951 the last of the Quadrant Brazils, Amy, was also dead.

A comfortable and successful life had come to an end. It is true that her books do not retain the appeal that they did in those days when class and position were rigid indicators of success. The language of her girls who had 'topping' and 'whizzing' ideas, now seems dated and comical. What can be said of her is that for someone who was brought up in an age when single women often led solitary and miserable lives, she broke the bounds by being both successful and involved in social life and able to amass an income which was far greater than some professional men of her class could hope for.

Bibliography
Brazil A., (1925) My Own Schooldays, Blackie & Co., London
Freeman G., (1976) The Schoolgirl Ethic, Allen Lane Penguin Books Ltd., London

Nellie Carter.

Nellie Carter was born in 1904, the eldest of three children. Her father, William Barnett, was a gardener at a local house in Kenilworth and her mother was the cook. He was undecided whether to marry Ellen, the cook, or Mary, the housemaid! However, he chose Ellen and Nellie was born twelve months later. Sadly, Ellen died in childbirth.

By this time Nellie's father had his own business as a market gardener. He took this small baby with him on his rounds, wrapped in a shawl, lying in a wicker basket strapped to the side of his horse. Later, while Nellie was still a baby, he married Mary the housemaid. They had two children, a girl and a boy.

Nellie grew up in Kenilworth and went to school there. She did well and on leaving, her first job was as a telegraph messenger with the Post Office. She delivered telegrams all over the district on her bicycle. By this time she was a keen member of the local Methodist Church, in Kenilworth.

The opportunity arose for Nellie to work for Parbury's the printers, in Coventry, where she trained as an accountant until her marriage. During this period she became much more interested in the work of the Methodist Church, as a Sunday school teacher and her work with young people. Much encouraged by her seniors in the Methodist Youth Department and the tutors at Westhill College, in Birmingham, where she attended for three years, after being granted a bursary, she trained to be a Youth Worker and eventually became a Circuit Preacher. This meant that she could be called upon throughout the Methodist circuit. Her first sermon was preached at Meriden.

When Nellie married Walter Carter, a painter and decorator, they went to live in Earlsdon, Coventry. The Methodist Church there was housed in what we now know as the Criterion Theatre and her husband watched the present church being built as he worked on a site opposite. The couple had one son who also went into youth work, firstly at the Central Hall, Birmingham and then at Runcorn. He is still working in the same field.

Continuing her circuit preaching Nellie was in great demand. She was one of the first women preachers and has many stories to tell. On one occasion she went to the McDonald Road Church to preach, wearing new shoes, she slipped and entered feet first!

Nellie is still an active member of Earlsdon Methodist Church, living quietly in the area and taking a keen interest in all that goes on around her.

Interviewed in May 2001.

Councillor Sheila Collins. Lord Mayor of Coventry 2000-2001.

On Thursday the 18th May 2000 at 10.45am, a fanfare of trumpets was heard from the Coventry Council House heralding a procession. Led by the mace and sword bearers the outgoing Lord Mayor and her consort, along with other civic dignitaries suitably robed, walked to St. Mary's Hall for the Annual General Meeting of the council. A short time afterwards the leader of the council, Councillor John Fletcher, led a second robed procession to the Guildhall consisting of the Deputy Lord Mayor Sheila Collins, the Chief Executive, the Town Clerk, the Honorary Recorder and members of the council. Councillor Fletcher knocked on the door and sought the consent of the Lord Mayor to admit the procession for the meeting.

After the meeting had confirmed Sheila Collins as Lord Mayor, for the civic year 2000-2001, the assembly processed back to the Council House where a reception was held.

Sheila Collins was born in the mining village of Horden Colliery, in County Durham where her father was a miner. In 1939 he brought his family to Coventry in search of a better life. Her father first worked at the Daimler Car Company, but a government call for miners during the war saw him return to mining at Coventry Colliery.

Sheila attended Radford Primary School until it was bombed and was then sent to Hill Farm. This too, received bomb damage. After a period without schooling she went to Keresley Grange and then on to Barkers Butts Secondary Modern School. On leaving she worked at the Daimler Car Company, in the accounts department and then moved to the Standard Motor Company.

In her leisure time Sheila was a keen sportswoman who enjoyed swimming, netball and athletics. She joined the Godiva Harriers Athletics Club competing in various athletic events. Although she confesses that she was not very good, she says that she helped others by providing competition for them. She is of the opinion that sport is character building and teaches team work and discipline. 'It also teaches you how to win or lose. That's most important; if you're a good loser you'll be a good winner.' Now, when she has the time Sheila is 'trying to play golf.'

Another of her pastimes was dancing and it was on the dance floor, at the Rialto Casino, which was in Moseley Avenue, (Coundon), that Sheila met Gordon Collins. They married and settled in Allesley where they still live. They have two married sons and one granddaughter.

Sheila and Gordon were totally committed to their family, but life was not easy for them. Gordon, who worked in the car industry, was made redundant four times over the years. To help with paying the mortgage Sheila took a temporary job, as a cleaner, at Jaguar Cars, which was just a short walk from her house. The hours fitted in with the childrens' school hours, which was most important, so that either she or Gordon were always at home for them. After a short time contract cleaners took over at the Jaguar and Sheila continued working for them.. Her upbringing and her father's influence has resulted in her holding strong political beliefs. She joined the Transport and General Workers Union (TGWU) becoming a senior shop steward, representing both men and women, for all Jaguar's plants. She admits that she was not afraid to speak her mind and did so often. Twenty-seven and a half years later she left, but not without having made her mark.

In 1986 Sheila stood for election to the City Council in the Longford Ward. She was duly elected and has represented them ever since. She says that she has always been treated with respect by all the councillors. Her interest in sport led to her becoming chair of the Leisure Committee, which was fortunate because there was a possibility that Coventry's Sports Centre might be knocked down. Sheila was very angry. 'I dug my heels in and fought like mad. I had a lot of support and was able to get two and a half million pounds capital into it.' She firmly believes that every child should learn to swim.

Sheila particularly enjoyed being chair of Planning, feeling that she could make a difference to people's lives in so many ways. 'Just to do a small extension to someone's house makes so much difference to quality of life.' Sheila was able to put forward a woman's point of view on planning ideas. She was also keen to encourage investors to come to the city. However, she is quite honest in admitting that mistakes have been made.

Becoming chair of Regeneration 'was really interesting. Coventry has always been very forthright in its thinking and visits were made, to see what other councils had done, to see if it would fit in with our city. We encourage a lot of investment.'

Coventry's lack of strategy in attracting tourists concerns Sheila, and she chaired the Tourism Committee. It worries her that after visiting the cathedral, visitors get back on their coaches and go to other towns such as Warwick and Stratford. As she rightly says 'Coventry has so much more history, we should promote our city.'

Sheila was also chair of the board of the Museum of British Road Transport. She has served on various Policy Teams, is a School Governor and also a Labour Group Officer. Her life as a councillor was and still is very busy.

The pageantry preceding Sheila's appointment was her choice, because she wanted to provide a spectacle for people and to emphasise the importance of the role of Lord Mayor. 'It is a privilege to be one of only twenty-four cities granted a charter bestowing Lord Mayoralty on them.' Becoming Lord Mayor of Coventry was the ultimate accolade for such a conscientious councillor. Sheila, with her husband Gordon as consort, took every opportunity of promoting Coventry's industries and culture. 'You forget politics when Lord Mayor' she says.

During her time as Deputy Lord Mayor Sheila had been given a dress allowance which she enjoyed using. When she became Lord Mayor she was required to pay all her consort's expenses. Only elected members receive allowances.

There were many highlights of her mayoral year, but each appointment undertaken was memorable in its own way. Close to home there were 'human highlights' as Sheila called them. Both she and her predecessor, Joan Wright, distributed Coventry Millennium Medallions to every school in the city and when Sheila was unable to, because of her incapacity, the Deputy Lord Mayor undertook some of the visits.

'I do believe in religion; I do go to church.' Coming out of Holy Trinity wearing her chain of office, Sheila felt a tap on her shoulder and turning saw an elderly woman who said questioningly 'You went to Barkers Butts and you played netball?' Sheila said she had done so then realised the speaker was Miss Parncutt, a former teacher of hers. Sheila asked her to say prayers at the Civic Service in Holy Trinity Church whose vicar the Reverend Urquhart, she had appointed as her chaplain.

A visit to St. Etienne was made in September, to commemorate the anniversary of the Battle of Britain. Sheila was able to fund two former Royal Air Force veterans of the battle, from Coventry, to attend the very moving ceremony at Roanne airfield. There they saw aeroplanes familiar to them from the war years, the Spitfire and Lancaster among them. Observing the reception the two men received, and their emotional response to the occasion, was reward enough for Sheila's generosity. This too was a 'human highlight.'

In October 2000 Sheila was forced to give up her mayoral duties for six weeks due to having both hips replaced. However, she was quite determined to attend the 60th anniversary commemorating the blitz of 14th November 1940. This ceremony was held in Broadgate and Sheila, still on crutches, led the two minutes silence in memory of those killed.

Meeting President Clinton on his visit to Warwick University was a very memorable occasion. Sheila was greatly impressed by his charisma and erudition. 'What a world leader! He kept his audience enthralled while speaking for over forty-five minutes on globalisation, neither faltering nor using notes.'

> Both the local universities were great for us; we had a lovely time with them. They included us in their programmes and we attended Coventry University's Graduation ceremony. What an honour to do that, because these students are our future politicians, decision makers, or world leaders. When the overseas students graduate they

do their tribal dances; it's fantastic. Coventry University is also good for the city. It brings in a hundred and twenty million pounds annually.

Among those invited to the Mayor Making ceremony had been delegates from Parkes, New South Wales, Australia with whom the city has a close relationship. Therefore a reciprocal visit was made the following January, which was unforgettable. Sheila and Gordon led a 70-strong delegation, including a football team, and they were there to toast Australia Day (27th January). 'It was fantastic; everyone was so welcoming and friendly.' There were so many civic and social events to attend, along with sightseeing tours. Looking for kangaroos at midnight was an entertaining adventure. They took part in a parade of cars and horse drawn carriages and visited schools and community colleges, where they distributed Coventry Millennium Medallions to the children. Some members of Sheila's family accompanied them and while there they all took the opportunity of having a much needed week's holiday, visiting the Great Barrier Reef among other places of interest.

Several of the football team were unemployed and a 'spin off' of the visit was that one of them was interviewed and offered a job in Australia, which he accepted; he returned there a few weeks later. This pleased Sheila greatly and since then another young person from the visit has gone out there to work.

Sheila was invited to Cork for St. Patrick's Day celebrations which included a civic ball. They were treated royally and thoroughly enjoyed their stay, but regrettably their visit was very short.

Sheila has strong personal beliefs and when invited to become a magistrate, her husband encouraged her to accept, so she became a Justice of the Peace in 1983. She fully approves of the democracy of the system whereby three magistrates hear the cases. She found the cases she had to deal with, when sitting in the family court, were harrowing. Therefore it was no surprise that during her year in office she chose children to be the beneficiaries of the Lord Mayor's Charities. The first was Boole House for abused children, of which she saw so many in the courts and the Friends of Hawkesbury Fields School for Disabled Children. Because, she says, 'children are our future.' The record amount of £18,000 was raised from an auction held during the Lord Mayor's Ball and from a fashion show. Sheila was overwhelmed by the generosity of the people who attended the events and those who gave their time and expertise.

These are but a few of the visits and duties which Sheila and Gordon carried out. The Appointments Diary was extremely full.

After an enjoyable, but exhausting year Sheila and Gordon were glad to get their lives back on track. Of her year as Lord Mayor Sheila says she was proud to have the opportunity to promote Coventry. 'I did not realise how highly the public of the city regarded the Lord Mayoralty, they do hold it in high esteem and I was privileged to serve them.'

A very public denigration of Coventry by the BBC caused Sheila to rise in defence of Coventry.

> I get fed up with people, Coventry people as well, talking their city down. My father brought his family to Coventry in 1939 from County Durham to give us a better life. I had a good education at Barkers Butts and I *have* had a good life. My father's dream have been fulfilled and it is this city which has given us this. We are second to none in Coventry and lead the way in many things. I believe the heart and sole of this place is its resilience, its ability to face adversity and come out fighting. The city sticks by its mistakes. It doesn't stay with one industry it looks for further and future industry.

Sheila is wholly committed to promoting Coventry, its people and its future, locally nationally and internationally. She loves the city and works extremely hard, endeavouring to improve the quality of life for its citizens. Always ready to listen and help where needed, Sheila is a hard line politician totally committed to local democracy.

Many thanks to Councillor Collins for agreeing to be interviewed in October 2001.

JOAN DAVISON nee GORE

Joan was born on the 1st June 1926 at 3 court, 9 house, Hill Street in Coventry. The midwife was very busy that day as there were two other ladies having babies at the same time. She was running from house to house, between Joan's mother, Mrs Nettleton who owned a sweet shop, just round the corner from their yard at the bottom end of Hill Street and Mrs Hodierne who was in labour round the corner at her house in Bond Street, also a sweet shop. Joan does not know who was the first born, whether it was June Nettleton, Joan Hodierne or herself, but the three of them were born on the same day. The midwife wanted Joan's mother to name her Elizabeth, after Princess Elizabeth who was born just over a month before her, but she preferred Joan.

The courtyard that Joan lived in was opposite Bonds Hospital, which Joan thinks at that time was a home for elderly retired men. There were big black iron gates at the entrance, where she could see old men (always dressed in black) sitting on the benches in the courtyard.

The entrance to Joan's courtyard was through an archway. There was a big square with three storied houses on either side. The toilets were in a brick building at the bottom end of the yard; at least they did have a key to their own loo. Pieces of newspaper were strung together hanging on a nail.

She cannot remember all of the families that lived in the yard. The Brindleys lived in the first house on the right. Mr and Mrs Davenport, a childless couple, lived in the corner house, most of the time they were quarrelling. The children in the yard were frightened of her and she would try and teach the children to swear. She was always dressed in black. Her husband always seemed a quiet inoffensive type of man, well dressed, smart and clean. Another family were the McGrorys and she thinks they had five or six children. The Ravens lived lower down, with their two daughters and next to them lived the Taylors, who had two daughters. Mr and Mrs Linforth lived further down and Joan thinks they had four sons and one daughter. One of the sons joined the Army and was sent to India; this was before the Second World War. When he came home he joined the Parachute Regiment and was killed in the landings at Arnhem. Joan's next-door neighbours were Mr and Mrs Cotrell they had no children. Also there was a Mr and Mrs Fazakerly with one son Billy, they lived towards the top end of the yard.

Joan's house had one room downstairs with a brick tile floor. On one side was a huge black lead grate, which was always kept shining. Under the window was a leather sofa, a sideboard stood against one wall and a wooden scrubbed table in the middle. Opposite the window was a pantry and next to that was what they called the coalhouse (imagine the coal being carried through your living room). The door to the stairs was next to the coalhouse; these led to the bedrooms. You had to leave the door open to see where you were going, as there were no lights on the stairs. These were scrubbed regularly as they could not afford lino or carpet to cover them. The first bedroom was where her parents slept and Nancy, the youngest child, shared their room. There was another flight of stairs, which led to quite a large bedroom without a door, with walls of whitewashed bricks. This bedroom was called the 'Topshop,' perhaps in the past it had been used by watchmakers or weavers. There were two large beds, one for the boys and one for the girls three in each.

Joan's brother Les was the eldest, born in 1914, then came Dorothy, Edna, Arthur, Norman, Joan and the youngest was Nancy. Joan wonders how her mother managed to bring up seven children in the house.

The water tap was in the yard. Mrs Radford, another neighbour, was always complaining about Joan's mum, saying, "That Mrs Gore is hogging the tap again." Joan's mother would leave a tin bath full of washing under the tap so the clothes were well rinsed. Monday was the traditional washday, but it was necessary to wash again on Wednesday. There would be baths of blue water and starch water on the floor in the living room. Joan thinks they must have had only one tablecloth, because on Monday it used to be newspaper on the table.

Her father always worked in factories on machine work. ' The Newdigate' pub was her father's local, just outside their yard at the bottom of Hill Street. All the men used to meet in the Bar and at the side there was a little room called the 'Snug.' Most of the women in the yard would race up just before closing time and go into the 'Snug' for a small glass of beer and a chat.

Joan's maternal grandmother, Mrs. Venn, lived in a house in Bond Street adjoining 'The Town Wall' tavern. Joan used to love to visit there and go into Gran's front room to look at all the lovely coloured velvet and satin ribbons; her grandmother was a milliner by trade. Joan's mother had five brothers and one sister. Gran's younger brother Horace and sister Annie both died tragically of typhoid fever within a few days of each other, Horace was about eighteen and Annie twenty. Uncle Jack was the eldest and a bachelor. He was a trained electrician and a bit of a hypochondriac, as he never seemed to be at work; he lived with Gran Venn. Next came Uncle Tom he was married with four boys. One was called Norman, who won a cap for England at rugger and during the Second World War acted as an interpreter. Unfortunately, his father committed suicide and the youngest boy Jackie discovered his body when he came home from school; he had gassed himself. His wife was Aunt Sis and they lived in Catherine Street, Hillfields in a nice house. Next came Uncle Bill who unfortunately stuttered a lot. He was a very good swimmer and won many cups and medals. His wife, Auntie Annie, was a homely person. They lived in Yardley Street, Hillfields, with their two daughters Annie and Muriel. Then came Uncle Ernie and Auntie Lil, Joan thinks they had four or five boys. She does not remember her Granddad Venn, she thinks he must have died before she was born. His side of the family were comfortably off. Apparently he was a gambler who lost lots of money and Gran would have to make up the loss with her millinery. Joan said her mother told her that Gran and Granddad Venn once ran the chip shop at the side of 'The Newdigate' pub in Hill Street. Joan does not know how long they were at the shop before they moved to Bond Street.

Joan's mother and her sister Annie were very friendly with a girl named Teresa Bertolli; she also lived in Bond Street. Her father was an Italian, he was very tall and sported a huge moustache. Teresa was quite keen on Uncle Jack but nothing came of it. She was a bridesmaid to Joan's mother and father when they married in 1913, at St. John's Church on the corner of Hill Street and Fleet Street. All members of the family were christened at St. John's Church. She can only remember going there a few times when she was very small. She did not like the smell of the incense used in the services, as it was a very High Church. Later she attended a Unitarian Church in Smithford Street; she went with her older brothers and sisters. The Rev. Lee used to take the services.

The whole family were educated at Spon Street School. She remembers being taken by her mother on the first day of school, accompanied by June Nettleton and Joan Hodierne along with their respective mothers. They were taken into the Headmistress's room in the infants; her name was Miss Walker. While she spoke to the mothers, the children played with a doll's house. A large coloured picture hung in the main hall, of fairies, with lots of little animals and flowers. Around the edge were the words "All Things Bright and Beautiful, All Creatures Great and Small." When the three girls were about nine years of age they went over to the senior school. Their first teacher was a Miss Millerchip, a very tiny lady. Their next teacher was Miss Holman, who also taught games. Both Joan and her best friend Beryl Hartley were very good at games and were always picked to represent their school in competitions. Joan went swimming every Monday at the Priory Street Baths. At the end of the swimming lessons she would walk round the Cathedral looking at everything.

Joan's eldest brother Les was very good at football and played in many local teams. When he was eighteen he turned professional and played for Fulham, so of course he left his home in Hill Street to live in London. Throughout the thirties he played for a number of other teams such as Stockport County, Bradford City, Carlisle United and many others. Edna, one of Joan's sisters went to work in a wallpaper shop in Fleet Street when she first left school. She burnt her leg badly on the old black stove, used to heat the shop. She left the shop and went to work at a factory behind buildings in Holyhead Road. The factory, owned by Mr. Lee, polished and sorted industrial diamonds. The stones were so valuable that if one of the hands dropped a diamond on the floor, Theresa Bertolli the forewoman, would not let them go home until it was found.

Les, the footballer, kept writing to his mother to urge her to move from the yard and get a bigger house. At that time he had met a girl called Amy and wanted to bring her home. However, he probably felt ashamed of his humble home.

Joan's mother and father eventually found a house to let in Sherbourne Crescent and they moved there in 1932. Joan's mum was sorry in one way to leave the yard, as there was such a community spirit. If someone was ill, in trouble or needed help of any sort, someone would always be there. Joan was about six years old when the family moved. It was a Saturday and she was told to go to the Rialto Cinema with her brothers Arthur and Norman; they were to take her to her new home afterwards. It seemed a long way to go, she thought "Gosh we are going to live right out in the country," as it was all fields along Holyhead Road as far as the Alvis Works, by the railway bridge. Anyway they finally arrived at 13 Sherbourne Crescent and Joan thought "Aren't we posh." Not long after she moved into the new house, building began at the bottom of the Crescent on a row of terraced houses. The Maltby family moved into number 35 including parents and children Ruby, Betty, Mary and Monty. Betty became Joan's best friend (and still is). Betty and her sisters went to Centaur Road School, as they had previously lived in Earlsdon, while Joan and her siblings continued to attend Spon Street School. They all had quite a long walk to their schools. Sometimes they would meet up on their way home and walk through what was known as the Chain Gardens. This was the name of a pathway, which led from the Chain Factory with allotments either side, to Holyhead Road just opposite 'The Holyhead' pub. Joan used to ask Betty if she could carry her school satchel, as she never had one. Joan's best school friend was still Beryl Hartley who she thought was lucky to live so close to Spon Street School and did not have the long walk that she did. On Saturdays Joan would go into town with her mother to help carry the shopping. On Sunday she went to the new Unitarian Church, which was opposite Northumberland Road by the Alvis Bridge.

Joan's sister, Dorothy, married Squib in 1937, after a courtship of some years. He worked in a shop called Lynes in Well Street; he started there at the age of fourteen, became the manager and stayed there until his retirement. Edna and Betty Peutrell, Squib's sisters, were the older bridesmaids at the wedding, wearing pink lace dresses, while Nancy and Joan were dressed in blue satin. The dresses were shortened later on and became their Sunday best. The marriage took place at St. Mary Magdalen's Church in Hearsall Lane. They went to live in Caludon Road; over by the City Football Ground and just before the outbreak of the Second World War they too moved into Sherbourne Crescent.

Joan was thirteen years old when war was declared on Sunday the 3rd September 1939. She was outside a house at the bottom of the Crescent when she heard it over someone's wireless (they must have had it on loud). At school the older children were detailed to assemble with gas masks. They were taken for walks into the countryside, which she enjoyed, as they were only allowed to be in school for a limited number of hours a day. The children also took part in air-raid practices. She left school in 1940 at the age of fourteen, the average age for leaving school and starting work, unless you had passed exams for grammar school. Both Joan and Beryl had been successful, but Joan's family could not afford to let her go.

She started work in the machine shop at the Daimler Factory in Radford, grinding threads on the fuse caps for anti-aircraft guns and also fraising (which is taking the rough edges off certain metals). Joan was there for a couple of months when her part of the factory was badly damaged by bombs in a night raid. She then went to work for a saddle factory in Little Park Street called Middlemores. This factory had also been badly damaged in parts. In the section that Joan worked in, half the wall had been blown away and all the protection they had was some sacking that over-hung the gaping hole. It was very cold as it was November and they had to stand on a brick floor. She worked there for a number of weeks, but her fingers were getting cut to pieces and her mother told her to ask for her cards. When she did, she was told that she was on important export business and would not be allowed to leave. Anyway her mother went down with her to the offices and demanded her cards, which she finally got.

In January 1941 Joan started work in a high-class gown shop in Hertford Street. It had been badly hit during the blitz of November 1940, but the windows had been replaced and like lots of other shops in the city they carried on the best they could. She had always wanted to do something like dressmaking, as she loved sewing. The vacancy was for a junior in the workroom, where they did alterations to the garments for the customers. The shop was called 'Helena's' and the owner was Mrs Margerreson. She was a very fashionable lady and always heavily made up. Initially Joan's weekly wage was ten shillings (50p), for working six days a week 9am until 6 pm, apart from Thursday when it was half day closing. When she went home and told her mother what her wages would be she said, "You won't get much pocket money out of that I'm afraid." However, she did have two shillings and sixpence for her pocket money. Her job for a few months was sweeping the workroom floor, retrieving all the pins from the bits and pieces of material, which fell to the floor and putting them back into tins on the worktable. She had to get to work a bit earlier than the alteration hands so that all was clear for them to start work. She would be sent out with bits of material to get Sylko to match. She performed the duties of a skivvy, including making the tea. After a while she was allowed to tack up hems and she had to watch what the alteration hands did. Sometimes they took garments practically to pieces to make a perfect fit for the customer. She worked there for nearly twelve months before she was allowed to use the treadle sewing machine. The boss called her into the office just before Christmas and she gave her a ten-shilling note, as a bonus, with which she started her Post Office Savings Account.

Joan finds it hard to believe that so many civilians managed to get through the War without any injuries, considering the amount of bombing raids that went on in the big cities. Sometimes they were in shelters most of the night, but would still have to go to work the next day. It was a Thursday night on the 14th November 1940 that Coventry was blitzed; a very cold clear night. Joan's sister Dorothy, her baby Pat and Nancy (Joan's youngest sister) were evacuated to Cheadle Hulme, where Dorothy's husband had a sister Marion, who lived in a pub. It was common for the sirens in Coventry to start wailing at about 7pm each evening. Joan's sister Edna, wishing to escape the bombing, usually cycled to Corley at night and stayed in the cellars of the 'Bull and Butcher' pub, kept by Mrs Piper. Edna's boyfriend Frank (who was later to become her husband) worked in a factory during the day and was on duty most nights with the Auxiliary Fire Service. Edna worked at the Renold Chain. Amy, who was Les's wife, moved from London to Coventry to get away from the bombing (Les was then in the Army). Like Joan, she did alterations for a living, in a dress shop called Willsons, at the top of Smithford Street.

Joan remembers the planes dropping incendiaries, pinpointing the many aircraft and machine factories in Coventry. Joan, her mother and Amy took refuge in a brick shelter opposite Joan's house during raids. There were no seats in these shelters, so they had to stand with some of their neighbours, listening to the explosions and thinking that soon the All Clear would be going but it was not to be. The Alvis, who made aero-engines, was not far from them, a target for enemy bombs. About 9pm Joan could hear a lot of shouting and the warden came running into the shelter telling them to evacuate the street, as a landmine had dropped in the back garden of the house adjacent to the shelter. Fortunately for them it had not gone off. These land mines were enormous; they came down on a parachute and were like a huge black barrel, about 6 or 7 feet long by 3 feet in diameter. The Wardens told all the people to get out of the Crescent, as the land mine could explode at any time. Joan said they did not know which way to run. When she looked towards the city it was just one red glow, as if it was all ablaze. Her father and brother Norman were at the end of the Crescent and said, "Let's make our way to Allesley." Then Amy said "Oh my God! I've left my suitcase in the shelter." She carried her make-up, silver fox fur (Les had bought her this as a wedding present) and a number of other items. She always took this whenever they went into the shelter. Amy and Joan started to go to the Crescent again and the wardens said, "Where do you think you are going?" After they had explained their predicament to one of the wardens, he said "Stay where you are" and he fetched it for her. They started to walk to Allesley, with other people who had the same idea. They had only gone a few yards when a bomb dropped at the side of a shelter on the other side of the road. Auntie Betty, her mother and a number of other people were in it. They were fortunate to get out, as it was almost completely demolished. They walked as far as Eastlands Grove, which is near Southbank Road, the wardens told them to get into the street shelter there, as it was too dangerous to carry on. They were stuck in the shelter until 5 am. One bomb exploded in a garden opposite the shelter, cracking the roof. It was very cold and they were shivering, as they were not able to move much. Joan said her mother must have been frozen as she had dashed out of the house with her slippers on, they were all cold and tired and just wanted to get out. One of the wardens told them to see if they could get to Southbank Road School, as there was an underground shelter there. The bombing had eased up a bit, so they decided to chance it. The house on the corner had been hit and water was cascading down Southbank Road where the water main had burst. They had to climb over debris and wade through water, when all they wanted to do was to sit or lie down. When they got to the School they found the shelter under the school playground was running with water, although someone managed to find some duckboards to put down. At least there were some planks for them to sit on and they were grateful for that. However, condensation was falling off the roof and dripping on their heads and necks, which was most unpleasant. When the wardens thought it was safe they told them to go into the classrooms and they would see if they could get the W.V.S van to bring them a cup of tea. The van arrived later in the morning and they had a slice of cake and cup of tea.

During this time Edna had cycled back from Corley to find the Crescent blocked off. She was frantic because no one could tell her where the family was. How she eventually found them Joan does not know. She went off again on her cycle until she managed to get some bread for them. Joan says she has no idea if they had anything on it.

The next day Amy and Joan walked into the city, as Amy wanted to see if Willsons was still standing. There was a scene of complete devastation; they had to climb over rubble and hosepipes, with water gushing out of them. There were lots of buildings still on fire and army lorries were everywhere, with soldiers who had been brought in to clear the rubble and unexploded bombs.

The next night they refused to go to the school shelter, as there was so much water down there, so they slept on the classroom floor and some people slept on top of the desks. None of them had been able to wash, but Betty and Joan found a bowl in the school kitchen, unfortunately the water mains had burst and they could not get any water. They took the bowl to the house opposite and asked if they had any rainwater and were allowed to use the rain water butt. They took it back to the school and had a wash. By the time everyone else had come to have a wash, the water was filthy. They decided they could not stand another night at the school and they finished up at Squib's mothers house in Kingsland Avenue, which was still intact, although she had no gas or electricity. She got food for them all from somewhere and cooked it on the fire. They slept there three or four to a bed, but at least they could rest in some comfort.

There were two severe raids in April 1941. On a Wednesday night a small bomb fell at the bottom of Joan's garden, which blew up the garden shed and the fowl pen, housing the hens that supplied the family with a few extra eggs to supplement their weekly ration. Most of the windows at the back of the house were blown out, so there was a lot of clearing up to do. The second raid was on the Friday, which was unfortunate, as Joan's sister Edna was marrying Frank on the Saturday. The Geisha Café, in Hertford Street, where the wedding reception was to be held had received a hit. They were told that it was so badly damaged it would be impossible to hold the reception there. The Geisha would still be able to supply the wedding cake, as that was made at a bakery elsewhere. Joan's mother rushed around trying to get some food, so the reception could be held at home. The couple were married on schedule at St George's Church, Coundon. Dorothy and Nancy had returned to Sherbourne Crescent and Edna and Frank went to live with Dorothy while her husband Squib was with the Royal Marines stationed at Scapa Flow.

Joan first met Chris, her future husband, in August 1940, while accompanying her friend Beryl Hartley to the Empire Cinema. As they were walking home, two soldiers were standing by a bus stop and they asked the girls what time there was a bus to Meriden. They said they did not know and carried on walking along the Holyhead Road. They noticed that the soldiers were not far behind them and when they reached Northumberland Road, where Beryl lived, they caught up with the girls and asked if they could walk along with them. Beryl turned off to her home and Joan told the soldiers that she lived quite a way further on. She could not really understand much of what they were saying as she was not accustomed to hearing an Irish accent. They walked with Joan to the top of Sherbourne Crescent and made arrangements to meet at the Empire Cinema the following week. Joan told Beryl that she had made a date to meet them. Beryl was not too keen, but Joan quite fancied the blonde one who had asked her out. At the time Joan did not know that Chris was only eighteen, nor had he asked her age, thank goodness, as she was only fourteen (she thought that if he knew he would not go out with her). She did look older and was quite grown up for her age. After a while Chris was moved to London with his regiment the 23rd 8th Belfast H. A. A. Joan wrote to him whilst he was there.

Joan was coming up to seventeen and she would either have to go into the women's forces or work in a factory. She wrote to Chris for his advice and he thought it would be better for her to go into a factory. He stayed a few times at Joan's house when he was on leave, as his troop was being moved around quite a bit to different towns. He had been in France early in the war. In May 1942 he had embarkation leave, as they were being shipped to India and then on to

Burma. He spent the rest of the war there. The soldiers out in Burma and the Far East called themselves The Forgotten Army, as there was hardly any news about them. Chris and a friend called Fred (who happened to live in Sherbourne Crescent) were both ill in hospital in Burma. Their troop had moved down through India and were shipped back to England whilst they were both still in hospital. When Chris and Fred had recovered they made their way through India and when they arrived at the last base the Sergeant said to all the other men "Whatever these two chaps want give it them," as they had both missed their ship. They moved on to Singapore to make contact with the hospital ships, which were treating British prisoners of war who had been interned in Japanese camps. Chris and Fred had to get on these boats if they wanted to get home quickly, so they helped to look after the sick soldiers. They finally arrived in England in November 1945.

Chris started work at the G.P.O in Greyfriars Lane and was then transferred to the Post Office Telephones. Joan and Chris were married on the 10th June 1946 at St. George's Church, Coundon and they lived with Joan's parents to begin with. Their first child, Robert, was born in Bassett Nursing Home, on the corner of Bassett Road. Apparently Joan's G.P. Doctor Hobson, was a partner there.

The landlord who owned Joan's parent's house also owned two houses in Three Spires Avenue. These had to be rebuilt along with a row of houses that had been demolished by a landmine. When the re-building was finished Joan and Chris rented one of these houses and moved in. It was here that their daughter Julia was born.

Chris worked for Post Office Telephones until 1975 when he suffered a stroke. He was in the Newsagents in Moseley Avenue when it happened. Sadly Chris died on 12th April 1980. His illness propelled Joan into doing something to help stroke victims. She was one of the founder members of Coventry Stroke Group, which was set up in 1977. The first venue for the group was Faseman House, Tile Hill, then moved to The Stonehouse in Allesley and eventually settled at The Wilfred Spencer Centre, Allesley Park, where it still meets.

Joan worked very hard for the Stroke Group and did a wonderful job mostly looking after the social side of things and anything else that was asked of her, until ill health forced her to give up. She still keeps in contact with the Group.

Interview took place August 2001.

Selina Dix

Selina Dix was born in 1859 in the town of Beeston, near Nottingham. Brought up by her maternal grandparents after the death of her father when she was three, she was educated at the local school. Her grandparents ran a commercial hotel and maybe this is where her interest in domestic science and hygiene first developed. The constantly changing clientele of the hotel must have widened her horizons. She completed an apprenticeship as a pupil teacher, before going on to a teacher's training college in Lincoln. Some time after completing her training she was afflicted by an eye complaint, so serious that it necessitated a year away from teaching. However, she overcame this setback and continued with her career.

In the early years she taught at Asterby Endowed School, in Lincolnshire and Queen's Walk Higher Grade School, Nottingham, before being appointed headmistress of South Street School in Coventry in 1889. At the commencement of her four year period at the school, she had a staff consisting of one certified and one uncertified teacher, two ex-pupil teachers and four pupil teachers, to control 273 children. Under her direction the school changed from an ill-attended establishment into one that earned the reputation for greatly improved attendance and good results.

From the outset Selina Dix found the school dirty and unhygienic. Poor drainage created an unhealthy environment. She tackled the problems with energy, making sure the school was cleaned thoroughly and disinfected with the liberal use of strong remedies, such as carbolic and a propriatary brand of disinfectant called Condy's Fluid. In a letter dated 8th September 1942 which she wrote to a friend, Iris Steel, she says that she was sent there to clear out the livestock, meaning bugs, and she certainly fulfilled her remit. Ventilation was improved in the classrooms, which was considered of great importance. Pupils were indoctrinated with the importance of personal and general hygiene.

At first many pupils did not attend regularly, despite being on the school roll. Fees had to be paid by the parents and many could not afford to pay, or did not think it was necessary for their children to attend, preferring them to be out earning rather than learning. Parents were reluctant to be assessed and have the fees waived, feeling that it was an insult or charity. In late August 1891 Selina Dix made an announcement to the assembled school, that fees would no longer be required, but urged those who could, to put the money into a savings bank or clothing club. Her efforts with both pupils and parents must have been very effective, for within a year of her arrival she was complaining of overcrowding to the School Board. Numbers almost doubled in her four years there and results increased from a pass rate of 27% to 96.6% according to the letter she wrote in 1942. As the finances of the school depended on payment by results, this must have meant a welcome increase in income. She was promised the headship of Wheatley Street School if she improved South Street.

Selina Dix took an active part in teaching. Her staff was fairly inexperienced, which necessitated teaching the staff as well as the pupils. An hour before pupils arrived at 9am, staff would undergo training. They also attended evening classes organised by the Science and Art Education Department of the Board of Education, South Kensington. The headmistress did not exempt herself from these classes, believing there was no end to the practice of learning. These classes benefited both teachers and pupils alike, as knowledge filtered through into practical lessons. Classes in domestic science were initiated in 1890 followed by instruction in first aid and home nursing by the St. John's Ambulance Association.

She was not afraid to stand up to authority when the need arose. Measles was a constant threat to the working of the school. Approximately every two years the school was closed down due to an epidemic of measles, a frequent killer at the time. The Ministry of Health Inspector often over reacted to the situation, in the opinion of the headmistress. She complained bitterly about it, pointing out that children were far more likely to catch the disease in the confined conditions of their own home or playing with those infected, than in school. She also complained about the conduct of the doctor for not removing his hat in her presence, however, he never made that error again.

When Wheatley Street School opened in 1893 the headship of the girl's department was offered to Selina Dix, who had greatly impressed the School Board with her innovations at South Street. Wheatley Street was a very modern school with facilities and equipment far superior to that of South Street. The school offered a basic education in reading, writing and arithmetic, but the headmistress was able to take her interest in domestic science a step further than in her previous school. These lessons included hygiene, cookery, laundry, diet and physiology. A flat was built later, where girls could practice running a household. The deep interest the headmistress felt in these subjects was reflected in her membership of the Institute of Hygiene. She possessed a diploma in cookery and was awarded a bronze medal in 1896 by the Society for the Encouragement of Arts, Manufactures and Commerce.

Every day she saw the effects of poverty, poor food and ignorance in Coventry, which was no different from any other large town or city. She often provided breakfasts for children, before the free school meals system came into being. She strove to change the situation through the young girls who came under her care. By educating them in the benefits of good practice, she hoped to influence the next generation. She did not neglect their physical welfare either, encouraging them to take part in games, swimming and gymnastics. She organised outings to concerts, visits to places of interest locally and geography field work. Broadening the minds of her pupils was high on her list of priorities, linking up with activities outside the school. They had connections with the RSPCA, the Children's National Guild of Courtesy and the Young Helpers League, and others of a similar nature, which would stimulate thought for others.

One of her crusades in the interest of children was that of the families of canal boat dwellers. She thought that children should not be allowed to accompany their parents on their travels, for it interrupted their schooling and they were frequently neglected or made to work too hard. She did everything possible to have the law changed, but despite giving evidence to a Commission of Enquiry at the Ministry of Health, very little came of it. She was not impressed by the attitude of the members of the commission and made her feelings plain to them.

During the First World War Selina Dix did a great deal to promote the best use of the food available. She demonstrated the practicalities of providing economical meals, in the school kitchen, to the mothers of her pupils. A Communal Kitchen was set up in Ford Street, one of the streets surrounding the school, which prepared meals for distribution to four other centres. She was a member of the local Food Control Committee as well as a member of the committee formed to administer the Education (Provision of Meals) Act of 1914. Not only were her administrative skills required, but her practical know how. Child refugees were brought from Belgium and cared for at the school and money sent abroad to alleviate the suffering of children effected by the war. In recognition of her services she was awarded an MBE in 1918. She also received a decoration from the Russian government.

Another cause in which Selina Dix took a great interest was that of special schools, for children with educational and physical difficulties. She had supported Corley Open-Air School from its foundation, as its committee chairman. Once its administration was taken over by the Local Education Authority, following the Education Act of 1918, she still maintained strong links with the school. In fact Wheatley Street School had a special section for handicapped children in its grounds during a later period.

She belonged to an extensive array of committees concerned with the lives of women and children. She worked actively for the Red Cross Society; visited poor people for the Prince of Wales Fund; she was a member of the national and local council of the NSPCC; War Pensions Committee; the Advisory Committee for Women's Employment (Ministry of Labour); the Housing Committee; the Women's Co-operative Guild; the British Women's Emigration Society and Women's Citizens Association. As if that was not enough she gave advice to school leavers and their parents, as the chairman of No 3. Committee, set up for this purpose under the Education Act (Choice of Employment) of 1910. She later gave evidence to the National Commission on Birthrate, on the training of adolescents. She was certainly a supporter of women's suffrage too, although not of the activities of the militants.

For fifty years Selina Dix was a member of the NUT, joining in 1891. She was elected to the National Executive Council in 1907. When women received the vote in 1918, the NUT asked her to stand as one of their candidates, but she declined the offer on the grounds of her poor health. She certainly should have represented a local ward in the city council, but was barred from doing so as an employee of the Education Department. Her work for the NUT highlights her interest in improving the lives of teachers. She was secretary of the London Council of the Benevolent & Orphans Fund for fifteen years until 1910 and continued as Chairman until 1942. Membership grew from 11 to 373 during her time with them. She helped raise money for the benefit of teachers who had fallen on hard times. She was a also a pioneer of the Teachers' Provident Society, founding the Coventry branch in 1900 with just seven members, which increased to 619 by her death. Many teachers were grateful for the advice she offered regarding pensions for their retirement.

She retired from teaching through ill health in 1923. Her health had never been good, but her energy and drive must have been phenomenal. She continued to support the causes close to her heart for many years after her retirement. She spent her final years in a Teachers' Provident Society home in Matlock, Derbyshire. In the letter to her friend, Iris Steel, a teacher at Frederick Bird School in Coventry, which she wrote just before her death in 1942, she stated that she was upset at the death of her sister, especially as the doctor had forbidden her to attend the funeral. However, she was still giving advice about how to fill in forms and her mind was full of memories of her years in Coventry.

Acknowledgements.

The majority of the information contained in this profile is taken from an unacknowledged and undated biographical article about Selina Dix in Local Studies, Coventry Central Library.

A newspaper article, again undated and unacknowledged in Local Studies.

Letter from Selina Dix to Iris Steel, dated 8th September 1942, Coventry Records Office access number 1891/1-2.

Kathleen Dixon.

Like many young women during the second world war, Kathleen Dixon played her part in the war effort. First of all she volunteered to train as a nurse, although the work proved too heavy and demanding and she was forced to give it up following a collapse. Back in Coventry she was directed towards the fire service, where she remained until the end of hostilities in Europe. She experienced the period of heavy bombing from 1940-41 in Coventry and remembers vividly the reactions of people to the strain of living through the air raids.

Kathleen left school just before her fourteenth birthday, but her mother considered her much too young to be starting work at that age. After a short interval at home she became bored and a secretarial course was arranged, to give her a skill to further her career prospects. She began work at the G.E.C. in 1938, then aged fifteen, as a shorthand typist in the accounts department. Her home at 99 Clay Lane, was damaged three times during the war, twice severely and once less so.

On the night of the blitz of 14th November 1940, Kathleen, her parents and an older sister were sheltering under the stairs as bombs rained down upon the city. As she says, "You could lose track of time in the blitz," but she believes it to have been around 2.30am on the 15th November. An A.R.P. warden called to the family through the doorless front of the house, to get out and make for a public shelter, as there was a delayed action bomb under their house. As they rushed out, another warden told them to go back, as it was too dangerous to be out in the streets. However, they ignored him and headed for the nearest shelter. As Kathleen looked back towards her home it was just a shell, she could see straight through it. They had experienced many night raids through September and October and even daylight raids, when machine guns as well as bombs were used, but nothing prepared them for the ferocity of the blitz.

The surface shelter they headed for was already packed as they squeezed in, carrying the compulsory bag containing birth certificates, identity cards and ration books, all items to identify a person should they be killed, or injured and unable to communicate. As they stood packed like sardines waiting for the raid to end, Kathleen's foot touched something soft on the floor. She realised that pressed against the wall, were the sleeping figures of children, so weary they managed to sleep despite the constant bombardment and vibration of the ground as the bombs impacted with the earth. There was no murmur from these sleeping forms. During a lull she could hear a woman address her husband saying, "Do you think you could go back for the budgie." Another voice added, "I wonder what happened to the cat?" Despite the desperate situation they found themselves in, they could still think of such things.

Later a stick of bombs came screaming down to earth and Kathleen felt sure that the last one was destined for their shelter, it seemed so close. It did fall nearby, but fortunately no damage was caused to their shelter. Suddenly a man's voice rang out loud and clear, "Eh! You should see muck out here." It released the tension and raised a smile on many a face. There was no 'All Clear' sounded, but as the morning broke and they no longer heard the planes droning overhead, everyone emerged from the shelter and made their way home to survey the damage.

Kathleen and her family made their way to the home of a married sister who lived in Wyken. Her mother seemed to have aged ten years overnight, from the strain and worry. When they arrived at her sister's house, they found her waiting anxiously for news of the family. She was so agitated before they arrived that she had sent her husband off on his bicycle to seek them out, or find out some information of their whereabouts. Coventry suffered terrible destruction that night from the huge number of explosives used. Later, when she joined the fire service, Kathleen heard stories of that night. One concerned a fireman on top of his turntable ladder, directing a jet of water on to the Owen Owen's store, which burnt out that night. He looked around to see what he thought was a red telephone box coming down on a parachute. He reported this by telephone to those on the ground and they all looked up at this strange object. It turned out to be a landmine, the first he had seen and never to be forgotten.

Kathleen and the family remained with her sister until late March of 1941, when their house was habitable again. They had only been resident a week or two when the second blitz occurred. The authorities had decreed that there should always be a person in the house delegated to act as a fire fighter in case of incendiary bombs, which had done so much damage in the November blitz. When the raid began, Kathleen's father sent them off to her sister in Wyken again. They had only been there a very short while when her father rushed in looking red and flustered. They wondered what could have happened to account for his actions. He told them that he was just coming down the stairs carrying an eiderdown, to camp out on the ground floor for the night, when a great lump of concrete came crashing through the roof and sent him sliding down the stairs. At least his fall was cushioned by the eiderdown. He decided to abandon the house to its fate and followed his family.

A tarpaulin was stretched over the roof to keep the water out and they moved back in, only to suffer a further raid two days later, which damaged the house so much they had to move out again. The G.E.C. was hit that night too, consequently work and home were disrupted.

Soon after this Kathleen began working as a trainee nurse at Manfield Hospital, Northampton. It was an orthopaedic hospital dealing mainly with emergency broken bones from traffic accidents and dispatch riders. They also had a large number of cases of T.B. hips and spines. As there was no cure at the time, patients could suffer for years with the disease. No wonder these patients could become grumpy and difficult in the circumstances. Kathleen much preferred the lighter atmosphere of the dispatch riders' ward, where at least they were certain to recover and rejoin their units. While nursing at the hospital, children injured in the raids on London began to be evacuated to Northampton and elsewhere. At first they had been sent home in plaster when the authorities needed the beds for military and air raid casualties, but the danger became too great as the heavy bombing continued. When these poor little waifs arrived they were in a sorry state, with their plaster casts full of maggots, their heads full of lice and their bodies bitten by fleas.

Kathleen worked on the children's ward, getting the children cleaned up, re-plastering their broken limbs and getting rid of the vermin. The work was very heavy, for the nurses did everything for the patients. Frequently Kathleen worked nights on the children's ward, when there would only be two Sisters on duty for the whole hospital. The Sister would come on her rounds to check that everything was running smoothly and receive reports, but otherwise the two young nurses would have complete charge of the ward. Children who had been operated on during the latter part of the day would just be coming round from the anaesthetic as they relieved the day staff, sometimes as many as five children would be in this condition requiring attention.

Each night when they went on duty they took in a basket of food, usually sandwiches, for a snack in the night. Generally they ate their food as soon as possible, for if they left it in the kitchen the mice would consume it before they had a chance to. There was no refrigerator or vermin proof cupboard provided for their needs. The biggest obstacle to getting their food would be a visit from the night Sister. They had to report to her in her room and therefore could not keep an eye on the sandwiches, neither could they take the basket with them, for discipline was very rigid. Many a time their snack was inedible, due to the inconvenience of the Sister's visit.

After a year in nursing Kathleen collapsed, due to the heavy work and was invalided out of the service. Back in Coventry with her family, she had to report to the Labour Exchange. Asked if she would like to join the Fire Service, as her shorthand and typing skills would be an asset, at first she declined. She really did not want to be in uniform again after a year of wearing nurse's uniform, she would have preferred a civilian office job. Her protests appear to have been ignored, for she was given her green card and directed to report to the Central Fire Station for an interview.

The Central Fire Station, in Hales Street opposite the Hippodrome theatre, stood in an area of Coventry that had received relatively little damage during the heavy bombing of 1940-41. Kathleen became a member of the newly formed National Fire Service at the beginning of September 1942 and remained with them until 1945 when she was discharged. The National Fire Service was a development of the Auxiliary Fire Service with company and divisional officers from the original pre-war Coventry Fire Brigade.

The women's quarters were situated in a terraced house in White Street, where women went for their breaks. One hot day in summer, as they were taking a break from duty, a scruffy black and white dog wandered in through the open door. One of the cooks took a liking to the dog and decided to give it a thorough brushing. Later when their sandwiches and tea came, they were thrilled to see that they had sausage sandwiches, a real treat from the usual limp lettuce leaf between two slices of bread. However, their joy turned to dismay when they opened the sandwiches to view the lovely sausages, they found them completely covered in black and white dog hairs. Although the women got on very well together, there were plenty of complaints that day.

G. Division Headquarters, the administrative side of the fire service, was moved to Dane Road in Stoke, which was very convenient for Kathleen who lived nearby. They took over the newly built Stoke Park School and turned it into an administrative centre. G. Division covered Coventry and the surrounding area, all the villages and farms between the city and Birmingham, Nuneaton, Kenilworth and Rugby. There were office staff, catering auxiliaries, telephonists and firemen all based at Dane Road. Although it was not a working fire station, it was always manned by firefighters and soldiers seconded to the fire service, from the army. The large playing fields at the rear of the premises, were used for practicing techniques of fire fighting and rescue. After Kathleen joined the service it was a quiet period, but the men kept themselves busy with these practice runs, in case of emergency. The soldiers who had been firefighters in the army, had to learn a great many new techniques to cope with a civilian situation.

Bomb rubble would be brought from the city and erected in realistic settings to simulate the rescue of trapped people. This helped to improve the men's efficiency and kept them occupied when times were slack. When they were not training, special events were organised as morale boosters for the general public. These included a 'Wings for Victory' week, a 'Navy' week, carnivals, etc., when money was collected to help the services. All sorts of competitions were organised for the same purpose. The grounds were used for these events and especially the static water tank, which stood near to the road. A greasy pole would be lodged across the top and the firemen would try to knock their colleagues off. Bets would be taken on how long the man would survive before ending up in the water. It was all great fun and the money raised went to a good cause.

The work that Kathleen was involved in, was sorting out the returns sent in by the outlying stations, the fire watching crews and dispatch riders. The country districts were manned by part-timers, who combined their work on farms with fire fighting duties when required. Harvest time put great demands upon these men, whose first priority was getting in the harvest to feed the nation. The administration had to make sure there was full cover at all times, which meant juggling teams about, to ensure that both jobs were accomplished. Amongst the returns that Kathleen dealt with, a name recurred on several occasions. Week after week she saw the name of John Dixon, a dispatch rider in the service, stating m/c (motorcycle) out of commission. Unknown to her, this was the man she was later to marry. However, they did not meet in connection with their jobs, but at a political rally they both attended.

Part of Kathleen's work took her to the vehicle repair garage on the corner of Walsgrave Road and Bray's Lane. The Transport Officer, Norman Brown, had been in the fire service for a long time. He was a real character, who kept the fire engines in good order with his team of mechanics, many of whom were members of Coventry City football team. He would complain when the engines came in damaged, remarking, "What's the good of a fire engine if it's in a ditch." Kathleen always enjoyed her visits to the garage, it was a change from being in the office and the men were so pleasant.

At the beginning of the war large cars had been requisitioned by the fire service to transport men and tow pumps to fires. With all their equipment hung about their person they could not get inside the cars, so they stood on the running board and hung on, completing their dressing as they sped along. When they returned from a fire their thick, heavy uniforms would be soaked through. Winter was the worst, when they became chilled on the way back. Bronchitis and pneumonia amongst the fire fighters were a huge problem to the officers. Once back at the station there were drying rooms, where uniforms were deposited, but it was a constant anxiety. These men were young and fit, but such conditions might effect anyone. Officers were older, but they usually attended a fire in their own cars. As air raids became less frequent the fire engines could cope without the assistance of extra cars and pumps, but the 6-8 men to an engine still had that same dash to the fire, dressing as they went along and the soaking clothes afterwards.

Kathleen worked a nine to five day at Dane Road, but the telephonists, laundry workers, caterers and men all worked a shift system. A new scheme was imposed after a while as an experiment, four days on and 48 hours off. There was a mixed reaction to the change, which meant long, boring hours in the company of their team, leading to tricks being played upon each other, pillow fights at night and raiding each others' dormitories. The soldiers amongst them actually preferred it, because the 48 hours off usually enabled them to make home visits. After a year it was abandoned. The soldiers left in 1944 when the invasion of Normandy began and by then Coventry had very few raids.

If the sirens went in the night Kathleen was required to report to her local substation in Marlborough Road, Stoke. None too happy at having to leave her warm bed, she had no choice, duty came first. There was nothing she could do when she was there, except perhaps make tea. It was a pity that women were not used more usefully on such occasions, they were certainly capable of greater action and responsibility.

Although Kathleen was very young at the start of the war she carried out the tasks allotted to her with a willing and cheerful attitude, as did so many. Without their devotion to duty, Coventry would not have survived such devastation. When asked if she remembered any member of the fire service suffering from, what in modern times would be called post-traumatic stress, she replied, "I don't remember anyone cracking up under the strain."

Kathleen Dixon was interviewed in May 2000.

Catherine Gray (left)
The first Stoke Park pupil to become a doctor.

Margaret Rylatt (below)
Visiting the site of the Priory Gardens excavations.

Jessie Sadler
Born during the Boar War towards the end of 1900.
Seen above enjoying her 100th birthday.

Kay Sweeney
Headed a group who saved Starley Road
from being demolished.

Antonia Hockton
Born 1968 in Coventry
Seen above working on a commission of a green man in 2000.

Mary Montes
Born in 1923.
The author of some eight books on local history especially Earlsdon.
Sadly passed away in 2007.

Peggy Richards
(Below)
Taught in schools in Coventry, Germany and Kenya.

Gertrude Billson
Enjoying a well earned holiday.

Joan Davison
(second right)
with her brothers and sisters
on the occasion of their
parents Golden Wedding.

Barbara Lea. (above)
1946 Northern Rhodesia where Barbara became a 'District Medico-Evangelistic Woman Worker'

Kathleen Dixon. (left)
Playing her part in 1939-45 war by being attached to the Fire Service.

Beryl Aylward
Born May 1906
Educated at Centaur Road
in 1932.

Nellie Carter (below)
seen here on the
left with her sister.

Winifred Merrick Barrow
Born in 1892.
Became headmistress of
Barr's Hill School in 1932.

Councillor Sheila Collins
Lord Mayor of Coventry
for the year 2000-2001
confirmed on
Thursday 8th May 2000.

Catherine (Kitty) Gray nee Howat.

Kitty Howat was born and brought up in Binley, near Coventry, the youngest of seven children. Binley was a village developed round a colliery. Her parents had migrated from Scotland and her father became one of the first miners to work down the new mine. There were only eight houses in the village at the time and they were quite isolated from Coventry. There was no public transport and people had to walk to the 'Bull's Head,' Stoke, for the nearest tram to town. In the late 1920s an enterprising coal merchant, Mr. Renshaw, would sweep out his open Ford truck and run a shopping service on Friday evening and Saturday afternoon and evening. This seemed very exciting to the children.

Kitty attended Binley Central School until she was fourteen years old. This was the school statutory leaving age, but promising pupils could remain to take School Certificate. When Binley came within the city boundary, in 1932, this facility ceased. Higher education for Kitty necessitated her transferring to Stoke Park School and after interview and entrance test, she was accepted 'on probation' for a year as a fee payer. Being very musical her father also paid for pianoforte lessons at school. At the end of the year Miss Michell, the Headmistress, reported to the Education Committee that Kitty should have been a scholarship holder, and advised her father to apply for remission of fees. This was granted, but at the end of the first term half fees were introduced, since it was 'noted he paid for music lessons.'

At school Kitty was interested in the science subjects and wished she could become a medical missionary. She was a Sunday school teacher and played the harmonium for the children's services and evensong, at the Mission Church in the village. She was encouraged in the pursuit of medicine by the Headmistress who acquired a prospectus and forms of application to Glasgow University. Kitty did not believe that admission to university could happen so she did not inform her parents.

When the letter of acceptance arrived, it was necessary to confess, her parents were astounded; the fees were beyond the means of a miner. As a member of the city council, her father explained the situation to Councillor Alec Turner, chairman of the Education Committee. Mr. Turner was sure a grant would be approved, but that was not to be! The Town Clerk, Frederick Smith, and Councillor George Briggs were so ashamed of the refusal that both approached her father with £50 each on a long term loan saying, 'Get your daughter off to Glasgow.' The unthinkable had happened and Kitty became a medical student in 1935, one of 25 women and 200 men. A year later her father applied to the Sir Thomas White's Charity, which mainly provided for the education of poor people. The sum of £25 per year was granted for three years. The first term's fees had been one hundred pounds!

Kitty was the first pupil from Stoke Park to qualify as a doctor. Her first post after qualifying was at the Glasgow Royal Infirmary, where she worked for one year. Following this she worked at the Glasgow Children's Hospital and then as a locum in general practice in Torquay.

In 1944 Kitty volunteered for the Indian Medical Service, working in the Indian Army Military Hospitals. Whilst in India she met and married Dennis Gray.

On returning to Coventry she was appointed to the Maternity and Child Welfare section of the Public Health Department, when Dr. Arthur Massey was Medical Officer of Health for the city. Later, under Dr. Clayton, the M & C W sections was amalgamated with the School Health Department. Kitty was appointed Medical Officer for Cheylesmore and Whitley, the first combined area. She made pupil assessment for education at special schools.

In 1950 Kitty's father, Alderman Joseph Howat, became Mayor of Coventry, but she said it made little difference to family life.

With the demands of the three young children of the marriage, and wishing to have school holidays, Kitty gave up her medical career. She became a teacher of special needs children at Alice Stevens School, where she had been medical adviser. She transferred to Whitley Abbey Comprehensive School, to be associated with non-certificate senior pupils. Here she initiated a work experience programme by approaching local firms to take older pupils, for one day a week, to gain experience of the world of work, such as building, hairdressing, working in cafes, etc. She also taught science and Nuffield 'O' level biology.

At Whitley Abbey School Kitty ran a table-tennis club and one year the team members 'swept the board' winning both individual and team trophies. The senior boys' team was the West Midlands champions. Coaches from the Coventry and District Table Tennis Association gave their very valuable services at the Monday club night. For several years she organised sponsored walks for pupils around the National Agricultural Centre's (NAC) grounds, in aid of the Royal Commonwealth Society for the Blind.

In 1947 Kitty joined Soroptimist International of Coventry where she has been an active member ever since. She has twice held the Office of President, in 1952 and again in 1986 and is the longest serving member.

In 1963 she was appointed to the Coventry Bench and was Chairman of the Juvenile Court Panel from 1973-76.

Kitty Gray retired in 1979. She maintains her large garden and carries on her activities for the National Council for Conservation of Plants and Gardens (NCCPG). Through Soroptimist International she continues her interest in United Nations Association and other committee work.

Interviewed August 2001.

Muriel Grimmett-Offley.

Muriel Grimmett-Offley, nee Johnstone, was born in Coventry and attended Briton Road School. On 20th October 1940 the family home was destroyed in an air raid. All the family, except her father, who was tied to Coventry by his work, was evacuated to Suffolk to stay with relatives. They returned after a few months to the Tile Hill area of the city and she attended Whoberley School. She left school aged fourteen and trained in secretarial work at Underwood College.

She worked in this field until she married Gordon Grimmett, a funeral director, in 1951. She had three surviving children and worked on the administration side of the business, thus gaining an insight into what was involved. When her husband died in 1982, she carried on the business and in 1983 reorganised the premises. In the process she made the decision to attend funerals herself. Although unusual for a woman to take this role, she felt it was a vocation and needed special dedication to understand the problems and emotions of bereavement. Unlike many funeral directors she actually stays with the congregation throughout the service.

In 1983 Muriel Grimmett-Offley was the first woman president of Coventry and District Funeral Director's Guild and in 1986 she became president of the Regional Guild.

She met her second husband, Ken Offley, when he visited the business in his capacity as an insurance agent for a company specialising in insurance for funeral cars and hearses, at a cheaper rate than local firms. He travelled from the company headquarters in Essex to conduct the business. After that they met regularly and finally married in 1987. He continued his insurance work until his retirement. Muriel decided to join her husband in retirement and sold the business. However, she finds herself in great demand at funerals, where her sympathetic approach has proved so successful.

She is an ex president of Soroptimist International of Coventry and a member of the Inner Wheel.

Interviewed 28th February 2000.

Antonia Hockton: Sculptor, Stonemason and Conservator.

Antonia Hockton was born in Coventry in 1968. Educated in Coventry and Kenilworth, she showed a marked talent for art from an early age and was determined to pursue a career in art when she left school at sixteen. She completed a two-year Art and Design course at Coventry Technical College and a one-year Foundation course at North Warwickshire College in Hinckley, before a Fine Arts degree course in sculpture at Sheffield City Polytechnic.

During a work placement at Lincoln Cathedral, between her second and third year, she became interested in conservation work. Each vacation during her final year, she returned to Lincoln to learn more about the work of repairing and conserving the fabric of an ancient building. On the strength of her enthusiasm and aptitude, she was offered a traineeship in sculpture conservation. She went straight to Lincoln on completion of her degree course in 1990, where she spent three and a half years learning the craft of stone conservation. This meant learning through practical work, cleaning and repairing the statues and fabric of the building. In the summer months this involved being out on the scaffolding of the west front, cleaning and preserving the stone. In the winter months, conservation would be carried out in the workshop, often cleaning and repairing carvings that had been removed from the building.

Antonia was the first woman trainee to be taken on at Lincoln, therefore she was breaking new ground. She met with mixed reactions in the workshop. Some of the masons were hostile to the presence of a woman, a couple were even abusive. Others were kind and helpful, especially when it came to lifting, for of course the work naturally involved a good deal of heavy lifting. This prejudice could be found in both young and older men, some just could not cope with a woman in a man's world. Her reaction was to make sure that she was the equal of any man and frequently pushed herself to the limit. During the time she spent in Lincoln she not only did her conservation job, she became the works archivist and photographer of the cathedral and its houses, developing and printing the photographs too. She also had to attend many short courses on recording and research, health and safety, stone conservation and carving, science based courses and training in archive work, some as far afield as Belfast.

At the beginning of 1994 she made a career move to France. Her competency in French was fairly minimal and she found it quite a challenge coping with the language and the new work practices. The company she worked for was based just outside Poitiers, where she lived for the sixteen months of her stay in France. She learned the new technique of cleaning stone with a laser and became an expert in the field during this period. She worked mainly on churches around the region, in particular Notre Dame le Grande in Poitiers. She also carried out work on several chateaux in the Loire Valley and on Amiens Cathedral in the north of

France.

Attitudes to women in the profession were very different in France to those in England. There was never any question of her having to do the heavy lifting that was required of her in England. In fact, if she was doing a job alone, a mason would be sent with her to do any lifting before she could proceed. Women had more equality in management she found, but Frenchmen did consider it strange that a woman would want to do a dirty job. She was considered rather masculine, because she often did tasks that a Frenchwoman would never attempt. She never minded being dirty and went to work in her work clothes, rather than looking chic on arrival and changing into overalls.

The masons found her a refreshing change from the norm, because she spoke to them and treated them as equals. She never experienced the slightest problem with the masons, they were wholeheartedly supportive. During her stay in France, the very first woman mason completed her course in Paris and worked for a while in Poitiers. The whole working environment was very different in France and Antonia realised that she did not have to think like a man. She allowed herself to become more feminine and when she returned to England in 1995 some of her friends were surprised by the change.

On her return she set up her own sculpture conservation company, originally in Sheffield and more recently in Ipswich. She has encountered some prejudice in this role as well and finds it extremely annoying, but in contrast she has received help on an equal basis from government bodies and the Princes Trust, in setting up her own business. She added another skill to her repertoire, when she received tuition in letter cutting from John Green, the well-known Suffolk sculptor. Over the years she has worked on many cathedrals, churches and several stately homes. She has also been selected for a number of public arts commissions in various locations around the country.

In the early years of being in business on her own account, times were sometimes very tough. Occasionally she was forced to take short contracts with other conservation companies to make ends meet, but as the years have progressed her reputation has grown and she is never short of work. In 1999 she embarked on a part-time masters degree in sculpture at Norwich School of Art, as she felt that she was drifting away from her fine arts roots. She is now receiving more commissions for her own work and being allowed a freer hand to develop her own style. In future she would like to concentrate more of her energy into her own work and ease off on the conservation projects. However, she will always be attracted to working on antique statuary in museums such as the Victoria and Albert, for the inspiration it generates in her own work and for the pleasure of handling and preserving beautiful objects.

Interviewed initially in 1998, text revised in 2001.
Antonia gained her Master of Arts degree in September 2001

Barbara Lea.

Barbara Lea was born in October 1918 at 1 Regent Street, Coventry, the first of three girls. She was educated at a private school in Queens Road, which was run by the Flinn sisters, who were her great-aunts; she attended there from 1924-1929. She then went to Earlsdon Elementary School. In 1930 she went to Stoke Park School in Brays Lane, after receiving an honorary scholarship, the headmistress at the time was Miss Michell. Barbara matriculated in 1935 and left school.

Her first job was in a works office at Humber Hillman as an office girl, she stayed there for ten months. Whilst there she bought a Humber bicycle for £5. This was with a discount! She then went to work for a company that made food-slicing machines in Parkside, Coventry. Following this she took a job at the Provident Building Society in Hertford Street. While there she used to park her bicycle at Warwick Road Church, behind which was Sibree Hall, with a small chapel attached to it. Through various influences, e.g., reading and girls' church missionary fellowship, she had become conscious of the plight of the people of Central Africa compared with those of England. Africa, with its poverty and diseases, obviously needed help.

Miss Lea went into this chapel when collecting her bicycle from the cycle rack on September 30th 1937 and felt called by God to be a missionary, overseas. She spoke to someone in the church about this, who said, "Wait, pray and you will know in due course if it really was a call." She could not get the feeling out of her head and on January 25th 1938, when her mother and father went upstairs to say "Good night," she told them that she felt called to be a missionary and work overseas. Her father said, "Of course we don't want you to go away, but if it is for that reason then we will not stop you," Her mother said nothing (Barbara wondered if she had been influenced by relatives of hers, the Flinns, who were watchmakers in Coventry). Her paternal grandmother and sisters were interested in missions.

Barbara had been to a 'Children's Special Service Mission,' this was on the beach at Nefyn, North Wales. This mission was similar to those of the Scripture Union Movement. They held events on the beach and she and three other girls won a prize each for building a strong sandcastle. Barbara also won a book called 'Four Brave Women.' When it was Barbara's birthday she asked for a book on Mary Slessor of Calabar in West Africa and she thinks that this could have influenced her for overseas work.

She told her mother that she would go into nursing; this was to enable her to do her missionary work. The decision whether to go into teaching or nursing was easy, the training for nursing was free, the teacher training had to be paid for. She applied to and was accepted to do her training as a nurse at the General Hospital,

Birmingham. Her training lasted four years, during which time the nurses were allowed half a day off each week and alternate Sundays, from 4.30pm. After tea Barbara caught a train and for the magnificent sum of one shilling and seven pence she was able to visit her home, go to church and return to Birmingham. She then did a course in midwifery at the Sorrento Maternity Home, Moseley, nine months in the home and six months on the district, which was attached to Heathfield Road Maternity Home, Birmingham. During her nursing and midwifery training she also did bible study correspondence courses, which were all done to prepare her for Christian missionary work.

Barbara and another girl, Merlin Cole, also from Stoke Park School, were sent to Northern Rhodesia, Central Africa. Merlin went in 1942, but Barbara who was younger, was ready in 1945. However, there were only a few boats for civilians, as others were being used by the military. She finally obtained a passage in May 1946. The women were in cabins and the men on decks. She was to become a 'District Medico-Evangelistic Woman Worker.' This was a new post, celebrating the triple Jubilee of the London Missionary Society, founded in 1795.

Off Barbara went with fourteen packages, including her bicycle and twelve Kilner jars of salt (this was to be used to replace the loss of fluid in hot climates). She sailed on the Winchester Castle and spent three weeks on the boat. It passed through the Mediterranean Sea and the Suez Canal, where the passengers were not allowed off the boat because of the troubles in Egypt.

At last the boat docked at Mombasa in Kenya and the passengers were allowed ashore. The most memorable impression of the port, were the masses of flies on the dirty shop windows. This was when she first stepped, albeit briefly, on African soil. Her journey ended at Durban, in Natal, which reminded her of Bournemouth from the sea, bright and clean. She was accompanied by senior colleague companions, the Rev. and Mrs.H.Barnes. Unfortunately, it was dark when they passed through the Drakensburg Mountains and by all accounts they are a spectacular sight. At Mafeking, they left the South African Railway and went on by Rhodesian Railway to Broken Hill, (this is now known as Kabwe) in Northern Rhodesia, stopping en route to take on water.

She arrived during the First Phase of the Union of Churches of some missionary societies at Mindolo, a mission ecumenical compound near Kitwe. This was the centre of the copper mining area. Barbara was quite lucky, as one of the missionaries had arrived by air, but he hated flying, so she was given the return ticket to Abercorn (now Mbala) in a five-seater plane. When she got near to Abercorn the pilot said, 'Look, there is Lake Tanganyika,' but she could not admire the view as she had her head in a bag! Once the plane had landed, there was someone to meet her with a Bedford truck and she was taken to a little hotel in Abercorn. Still feeling a little sick she lay down to rest, then ate a good meal, before the twelve-mile journey to Kawimbe. Kawimbe is the oldest existing missionary station of the London Missionary Society in Zambia. It was founded in 1887.

Barbara had first to learn the Mambwe language; the name is Chimambwe (this means the language of the Mambwe tribe). She went away for four months to study. Remember there was no dictionary or grammar books in the language. She used the grammar book of a neighbouring language, plus the Mambwe New Testament.

Following this she was sent to a hospital in the north west corner of Northern Rhodesia, at Mbereshi London Missionary Station, to get some experience of nursing in Africa. From here Barbara went to the Plymouth Brethren Hospital in the Congo, to study eye diseases. She then returned to Kawimbe to start work in the little 'St. Anthony's Hospital' which had a maternity ward with eleven beds and six cots and an outpatients department which was very much in demand. The building was long, made of sun-dried bricks with a grass and thatch roof. The latrines were outside. Barbara was in charge and she was fortunate to have an African orderly who did know some English. There was also accommodation for nurses, a food store and an outside kitchen, where relatives could cook for patients. There was a Government Hospital, with a doctor twelve miles distant, along a rough unmade road.

Prayers were said each morning in outpatients and each evening in the wards. Ante and post-natal and child welfare clinics featured prominently. General medical and minor surgical work as well as administration kept Barbara busy. The diet of the Mambwe tribe was based on millet rather than maize. There was less malaria in the area, which was beneficial to their health. The maternity cases were straightforward, with few complications, possibly due to their diet. Medicines were available through the Government Medical Department at reduced rates, these were supplied in a basic form and had to be made up by Barbara.

Barbara had taken her first language examination six months after her arrival, at which she was successful. In preparation for her second examination at the end of two years, she went away for further language study. The subject she chose for her thesis was, 'The Mambwe at Work and Play.' She went into the villages to gather knowledge and experience of the way people lived, to enable her to write the thesis. This forced her to speak and be understood in Chimambwe. Communication with patients, nurses and midwives in training and the leading of church worship all required a good knowledge of the language. There was a Chimambwe Hymn Book, New Testament and Psalms and a booklet of Old Testament Stories.

After five years in the hospital and a leprosy village about a mile away, Barbara was pleased to welcome help with language study and hand over the hospital and leprosy settlement to an English missionary from China, (the

Chinese government refused re-entry permits to many expatriates in the early 1950's). This allowed her to begin the district work for which she had been appointed. By now she was familiar with the landscape and the villagers knew her. After a spell of meeting village headmen and church leaders, three village clinics were built for Barbara to visit by bicycle. She had help from church people, fetching water, mudding floors and assisting in treatments, for ailments like chest infections, abdominal, skin and eye complaints, malaria, injuries and in anti-natal and post-natal clinics. Before returning to the mission station, she met with local women for fellowship and worship. She ran nutrition classes for the Women's Fellowship. This Fellowship entailed teaching literacy, pastoral work and training the African women to visit the sick. The local Kawimbe women had started to hold their own meetings in the villages by 1956. The Fellowship was part of a nationwide organisation called 'KBBK,' i.e. Christian Women Helping Each Other, in the United Church of Zambia. It had its own uniform and badge.

For the first fifteen years, village visits were made exclusively by bicycle, these journeys extended up to twelve miles, with rucksack, etc. Upon seeing women in their 'fields' Barbara would go over to chat, not so easy from a Lambretta or Honda, let alone a car. Then her transport was augmented with a scooter and later a VW 'Beetle.' The latter enabled her to take women Fellowship leaders with her to other far-flung church centres, where there was a road. These leaders would encourage others to start meeting for growth and evangelistic witness.

Barbara's mother died in 1974. She came home for the funeral and then returned to complete her term, at the end of which she decided to return to England to look after her father. She has been back to Zambia twice, once in 1982 and again in 1993 and seen great changes, some encouraging and some distressing, the latter in the political and economic fields. She was in Africa for thirty years, obviously doing an excellent job with those less fortunate members of the world's population. Barbara continues to have her great faith and keeps in touch with her African colleagues through letter writing and prayer.

I would like to thank Barbara for letting me interview her, she has led such an interesting life and has done such good work.

Interview took place on the 28th June 2001.

Miss S.W. Michell

Sarah Winifred Michell was born in Cornwall in 1891. She graduated in history at Bedford College, University of London in 1914. She taught at the Lilley Stone Foundation, Newark-on-Trent and Sheffield Girls High School, before being appointed as the second headmistress of Stoke Park School.

The school had been founded in 1919 and occupied a house called 'Harefield' in Brays Lane, Stoke, Coventry. Entrance examinations were held on the 14th January 1919 and by the 20th January, eighty-seven pupils entered its classrooms. A third of the initial intake transferred from Barr's Hill School, as did a couple of teachers. Links between the two schools were very strong. Fees had to be paid, despite its being a local authority school. Miss Helen Scott was the first headmistress, who set a high standard and encouraged her girls to aim high in their ambitions and stay on at school as long as possible. In 1927, the year after Miss Michell's appointment, the first ex-pupil received a first class honours degree in botany, from Manchester University.

Miss Michell introduced several innovations to the school following her arrival. She initiated the house system, with the school divided into four houses, colour coded for instant recognition, to create a sense of loyalty and competition in the school. Each house had its own personal charity, to which it subscribed any money raised. Sports and educational competition spurred the girls to greater efforts. The prefect system, which she also introduced, worked towards better discipline in a rambling school building. Teachers and headmistress were always on duty and prefects supported them in making sure rules were obeyed and discipline maintained. A third innovation was the introduction of a school magazine. It was entitled 'Microcosm,' with its first issue on 19th November 1927. The aim was to foster literary talents in the pupils, with the opportunity for every girl to make a contribution at least once during her period at the school.

Miss Michell worked closely with Miss Barrow of Barr's Hill School, to upgrade the status of the two girl's schools. The local authority called them higher grade schools, but that was not good enough for Miss Michell and Miss Barrow, they insisted they should be called grammar schools. They fought hard to gain parity with the boys of Coventry. They did not always receive the support from parents that they expected. Miss Michell complained of the mercenary motives of parents who wished their daughters to leave school at the statutory leaving age, instead of staying on until at least sixteen. The local authority usually backed the parents when appealed to. The two boys' grammar schools were independent of the local authority and were housed in spacious buildings, with room for expansion and extensive grounds. The two girl's schools suffered severe overcrowding as they became more popular.

An extension was built at Stoke Park School in 1926 to house a gymnasium, laboratories for physics and chemistry, a library, domestic science room, a kitchen and five extra classrooms. It was possible to accommodate up to 300 pupils, more than doubling the capacity of the school. Despite this expansion early in Miss Michell's headship, as the years went by overcrowding continued to cause problems. Break times had to be staggered to ease the pressure on the cloakroom facilities. She continued to press the local authority for a new purpose-built school in the area. She was disappointed to discover that Stoke Park was only ninth on the list of schools requiring renovation or rebuilding.

By the 1930's a new school, being built in Dane Road, Stoke, was earmarked for their use. It would accommodate 500 pupils and would be ready by September 1939. Unfortunately they were destined not to occupy that building for many years, due to the outbreak of war. The almost completed school was recquisioned by the Warwickshire Fire Service as their headquarters in Coventry for the duration of the war. During their occupation, they knocked down walls to allow easy access for fire engines, and erected others.

Miss Michell and her staff working with the Barr's Hill staff, must have had contingency plans for evacuation in the event of war, for the day after the declaration of war 237 girls from the two schools moved to Leamington Spa. They shared the facilities of Leamington Girl's High School with the existing pupils, Leamington in the morning and Coventry in the afternoon. The Stoke Park and Barr's Hill girls met for assembly each morning at Dale Street Methodist Church hall. A couple of rooms below the hall were used as classrooms and when the weather was good they were taken out on expeditions.

The greatest concern of the two headmistresses was the continuity of teaching for their sixth form girls. It was imperative for them to study hard if they were to pass examinations and progress to places at university. They were determined not to let it effect their pupils' future prospects and every effort was made to facilitate their ease of study. Back in Coventry, schooling went on for the pupils who did not join the evacuation, although a shortage of teachers often meant part-time schooling. Only the lower floors were used as it was thought too dangerous to use the upper floors. Air raid shelters were erected in the grounds, for the safety of the pupils and staff.

As the period of the 'phoney war' progressed, parents began to expect their daughters to return and some drifted back to Coventry, much to the dismay of both the teaching staff and the local authority. Eventually they bowed to parental pressure and the school returned in the autumn of 1940. The first Speech Day following their return was held for the upper school only, at their old assembly hall in Brays Lane on the 14th November 1940. Miss Michell told parents that the return had been against the wishes of the staff and the local authority and she hoped that they would not regret their decision. What prophetic words they were, for that was the night of the terrible blitz that hit Coventry and virtually destroyed its centre. Almost immediately plans were made to evacuate the two schools again. This time it was to Atherstone that they retreated. The headmaster of Atherstone School, anticipating the need for extra classrooms to accommodate evacuees, had extended his school. Miss Barrow took charge of the 237 girls who spent the rest of the war in Atherstone, while Miss Michell remained in Coventry.

When the war ended and the pupils returned, overcrowding became a pressing problem again and there was no immediate relief. Work had to be done on the Dane Road premises to remove the baffle walls that had been erected and restore the building to its original purpose. As a temporary measure, Nissen huts were placed in the garden at Brays Lane to accommodate increasing numbers, as families returned to the city. Miss Michell also found difficulty acquiring enough staff to teach the growing numbers. At first, classes were held at Dane Road and Brays Lane, until the Dane Road site was fully functional, more than a year after hostilities had ceased.

During Miss Michell's twenty-one years as headmistress of Stoke Park School the sixth form increased from just five to sixty in 1947. Girls had gone on to gain degrees in medicine, theology, mathematics and many other subjects. She thought no career was unobtainable for her pupils, if they worked hard at their studies. In fact she stated that there was a need for more women barristers, doctors, surgeons, social workers and architects. To quote her own words.

> Our country needs women of the highest intellectual ability, combined with great moral integrity, if it is to maintain its place in the world and continue to give the lead in such spheres as medicine and democratic government.

The ethos of the school was work and service. The girls were trained to use their brains and serve the community. The school motto Servire est Regnare (To serve is to Reign) reinforced this attitude. The house system, with its emphasis on charity work in the local community and the wider field, gave them a feeling of responsibility to others and broadened their minds. In fact many pupils became nurses and a few became missionaries. The character of the school reflected Miss Michell's own personal conviction. She had a strong religious belief, which was illustrated in her membership of the Coventry Council of Churches and in her involvement with Coventry Cathedral and its pageants. She also did much to promote the role of women, by representing the Coventry branch of the National Council of Women, on the Education Executive in London. She was also a member of the Coventry Education Committee.

When she retired in 1947 she returned to her home county of Cornwall, where she settled in Penzance. She always kept in touch with old friends and colleagues from Stoke Park and kept herself up to date with progress in the school. She was vehemently opposed to the comprehensive system, believing it to be a retrograde step in education. When she was interviewed in 1970 her clarity of mind was remarkable, when recalling her time at Stoke Park School. She lived on in Penzance until her death in 1982.

Acknowledgements.
Dr. Kenneth Richardson audio tape collection, Coventry University Library.
The House in the Park; The Story of Stoke Park School. Stoke Park History Group.
Coventry Evening Telegraph.
Twentieth Century Coventry. Dr Kenneth Richardson.

Mary Montes

Mary Montes, writer of some eight books on local Coventry subjects, particularly Earlsdon and the watch making industry, is a person who likes the noise and bustle of urban life. Not for her the peace and quiet of the countryside, except perhaps, for a day out. She likes the fact that 'buses pass her window and that she can hear peoples' voices as they walk past her flat in Dalton Road. Mary was born in Poplar Road, on the 21st October 1923 significantly the anniversary of the battle of Trafalgar. She has had a life long interest in history, which is not surprising, since her father taught her to read before she went to school from a very old copy of a book called, 'The History of England'. The school she attended was of course Earlsdon School. At the age of eleven years she passed the scholarship for Barr's Hill School. Unfortunately, not only was her schooling interrupted by the war, but her mother was constantly unwell and she had to have lots of time off school to look after her. An ultimatum came in the form of a letter from Mr. Harrod the Director of Education, 'Attend school or leave', and so she left. After her mother's health had improved Mary went to work at A.C Wickman and that started her career in office work. Towards the end of the war Mary went into nursing and it was at this time that she met and married her husband. She had a daughter Anita and a son Paul.

In 1979 the Earlsdon History Society was formed, as a result of the 135th anniversary celebrations of the founding of Earlsdon. Mary was an enthusiastic member. It was also in that year that the Earlsdon Echo Newspaper was started and edited by Graham Partridge, as it is still.

Some time after this Mary left Coventry to live in Kent with her cousin, due to unhappy circumstances at home. However, after six months away she was missing her friends in Coventry and so she came back to live in Earlsdon, as Mary calls it, 'the location of my roots'. She soon found a flat and settled down.

One of the first people she met on her return was her good friend Bill Dunn and she joined the Earlsdon History Society. After a couple of years, with significant people leaving Coventry and the Society, it slowly declined and Mary seemed to be the only one doing research, eventually the group fizzled out completely. Mary carried on with her research, because she had become deeply interested and involved in the history of Earlsdon. However, she felt that to continue this research she needed in depth knowledge of the watch making industry; as the two, Earlsdon and the watch making industry, were inextricably linked. It was the watchmakers who had founded the school and the church there. Reluctantly Mary set about the complicated business of finding out how watches were made. When she got started on her research, Mary found it very rewarding. As she says, 'Although I have lived in Earlsdon all those years, had been born there and grown up there, I had no idea, until I joined the Society, that there was such a thing as the watch making industry in Coventry and particularly in Earlsdon'.

Mary had written one or two articles for the Echo, but she felt she wanted to write something more substantial; so her first book was a history of The Earlsdon Cottage public house. The idea behind this was that the book would be sold in the pub, where customers were readily available. So Mary wrote and published the book herself. It was printed by an Earlsdon printer (who else?) with premises on the corner of Moor Street and Warwick Street. Mary was right, it did sell very well, particularly in The Cottage and has been reprinted twice.

The next book was 'Brown Boots'. This started as a fairly long article for Warwickshire History Publications, but Mary felt it could be expanded into a book. This was published by the Historical Association, of which she was and still is, a member. This book has also been reprinted twice. Called 'Brown Boots' because although the watchmakers may have had times when they were short of money, they kept up appearances with their brown boots.

In 1985 Mary published a history of St. Barbara's Church. For the 100th anniversary of Earlsdon School she decided to go through the logbooks, and to take an entry from each year to make into a book; with comments, if possible, by someone who had attended the school at the time. This was something she enjoyed doing very much. Mary would like to see this book reprinted for the 150th anniversary of Earlsdon in 2002. For this anniversary an exhibition of paintings by Earlsdon artists is to be mounted, hopefully, at the Herbert Art Gallery. It is also hoped that there will be an exhibition in Earlsdon of photographs and artifacts, amongst other celebrations.

Mary's latest book is the 'Earlsdon History Trail', which was to celebrate the millennium. This was initiated by Mary and a small group of Earlsdon people. They decided that plaques should be put on buildings of interest. Mary suggested twenty buildings and wrote a short inscription for each plaque. The plaques, together with a book giving a short history of each building makes a very satisfactory tour of Earlsdon. The walk was inaugurated by the Lord Mayor, Joan Wright and Jim Cunningham M.P., and led by Mary. This is only one of several walks that Mary has initiated because as she says, 'Earlsdon has such a fascinating history crammed into the past 150 years'.

Mary meets some very interesting people at the talks she gives, particularly in connection with the watch making industry. People often come to tell her that their grandfather was a 'watch jewel hole maker' or a 'watch finisher', because the making of a watch had many different operations before it was finished. She finds speaking to these people rewarding and feels that she has helped to revive interest in Coventry's watch making industry. This industry was, she is sure, the foundation of many of Coventry's subsequent precision engineering industries. These men brought their skills, learned in a seven-year apprenticeship, to many other companies, after the slump in the watch making industry. Mary retains a strong interest in the Coventry Watch Making Museum Project. The group hopes to find a permanent place to house the records and artifacts they have collected.

A future project Mary has in mind, is a history of Coventry's cinemas. This was started by Bill Edkins, who was the owner of the Imperial, later Continental cinema. At one time there were more than twenty cinemas in Coventry. Bill Edkins always hoped that Mary would take on the project. He has now died, but his wife, who holds the material, would very much like Mary to turn this material into a book.

When the Earlsdon Society became defunct, Mary became the guardian of the collected archive, this together with her own researches, has become quite a large collection. Mary revived the Earlsdon Society in 1998, so now the archives have a permanent home in Earlsdon. The Society has a dedicated following, so this unique collection is in safe hands.

Not only is the collection unique, but Mary herself is unique. By her publications, talks, and the exhibitions she has helped to arrange, she has been in the forefront of bringing Earlsdon's history, and the watch making industry to the notice of so many people.

Interviewed September 2000.

Marguerite (Peggy) Richards.

I was born in March 1914, the first of two girls, in Stoney Stanton Road, Coventry, where we had a shop next to St. Mark's School. I attended this school until I won a scholarship to Barr's Hill School. The head teacher at St. Mark's, Mr. Jacques, was a tall, courteous, God-fearing man, who believed in the world of the Old Testament and was definitely into Darwinism. Barr's Hill School was something of a culture shock in the days of that formidable Victorian bluestocking, Miss Grace Augusta Howell and her staff, mostly made up of the generation whose putative husbands were buried in Flanders. In the mid-twenties we still had Christmas parties for wounded soldiers at High Cross, a nursing home next door to the school, for those men recently moved from other hospitals.

I remember most of the Coventry Mystery Play and the year of the Godiva procession of 1929. We had a tableau on a float and I was the plump and footsore abbot who had to walk beside it. Muriel Mellerup played Lady Godiva, in body tights and a prodigious mass of hair, probably augmented!

I trained as a teacher at Fishponds Teacher Training College, Bristol, from 1932-34. This was a time of cuts, when teachers and public servants (including King George V) forfeited 10% of their salaries. I took art as my main subject, a life long interest. I began teaching at Cheylesmore Infants and Junior School, under Edith Walker, who was original, inspiring and years ahead of her time, unfortunately her successors were not. She died much too early, but her influence was deep.

In the few years before the war, times were unsettled, Hitler and Mussolini were in the ascendance. No one believed Chamberlain's "Peace in our time", but we all wanted to. In 1939, my sister and I returned early from a holiday, to be confronted by the wreckage of the I.R.A. bomb in Broadgate and were hustled on by the police as we were carrying suitcases.

We were recalled early to our respective schools, to contact parents with evacuation plans. We all lined up at Coventry station with cases, gas masks and labels, bound for Atherstone. I remember the line-up at our destination, a bit like an auction! Needless to say, the children were snapped up first and the teachers drew the short straw! I finished up with a mixed group at Mancetter Village School, with a less than enthusiastic Head teacher. We stayed through a heavy winter of snow, followed by floods, in the period the Americans called the 'Phoney War'. By Easter, many of the children had returned home and the remainder absorbed into the village school. Cheylesmore School, being near the railway, remained closed as it was thought unsafe. However, by the summer, after teaching in people's houses for some weeks, it was reopened and then the raids began. The school was bombed in October and we were lodged in St. Michael's

School.

In the November 1940 raid, I was in a brick shelter outside our house in Forfield Road, when we received a direct hit about midnight. We heard the first three bombs of the stick, but not the one which struck us. My father said, "This is ours" and stood up. He had on his fireman's helmet and was not totally buried, as we were. All went very quiet and then a second fall, as the blown up debris came down. I heard my father calling for help to get us out and soon neighbours and wardens came to our aid. My friend who lived next door was badly injured and as a consequence paralysed. My ankle was smashed and the foot pointed the wrong way. When we were uncovered it was brilliant moonlight and hoar-frost was already forming on the bricks. A sixteen-year old messenger boy, whose only driving experience was motor-cycling, found an abandoned bus and managed to drive it to Allesley School First Aid Post, where doctors and nurses were working frantically all night, with little equipment. As daylight dawned, we were taken in makeshift 'ambulances' touring the county for vacant beds. I spent the rest of the winter in Warwick Hospital. For the remainder of the war I was teaching at Moseley Avenue School.

In 1947 I joined the British Families' Education Service in Germany, a founder member in fact, and opened a school for the children of servicemen at R.A.F. Lubeck. I lived in the officers' mess and had two rooms in Station Headquarters for a school, again very makeshift. After a dreary wartime of restrictions, my lameness improved and it was wonderful to be able to see so much of the Continent. We were allowed some travel concessions and managed to 'find' ourselves a few more. Social life was decidedly brisk, but I felt that I had earned it. The following year I opened a new school in Kiel, in a large house with a garden and given a free hand in equipping it. Make do and mend again, but quite exciting.

In 1949 I joined the Colonial Service as a teacher in Nairobi, another culture shock! The schools were segregated then and run on pre-war prep school lines, somewhat less than progressive. The school was half day and half boarding. I was head of the East Block for older girls and younger boys. I joined the cathedral choir, again all European. I managed to tour the Congo and visit Zanzibar and Pemba and saw quite a lot before the troubles began in Kenya. There were rumblings of trouble for over a year before the Mau Mau raids started. Animals were hamstrung first and then the outlying European farms were attacked. Lari, where the able bodied men all worked down the railway line and were away all day, was literally 'put to the sword'- the victims being old men, women and children. This village had not taken the Mau Mau oath to kill all Europeans.

At the end of my tour of duty, I returned to Coventry and in 1954 I became Head teacher of Hill Farm Infants School, where I stayed until I retired in 1977. In 1962 I married Dick Richards, a fellow Head teacher and acquired a step-daughter, Vicki. We opened a unit for the 'partially hearing', which was very interesting. Having a very deaf father-in-law living with us, had made me very conscious of the need to integrate the deaf into mainstream schools. After I retired I concentrated on painting, particularly after I lost my husband in 1981.

Thank you to Peggy Richards for this contribution.

Peggy Richards, now an invalid, lives in retirement, but still takes a lively interest in everything, both locally and nationally. She pursues her hobby of painting, taking her equipment on her motor scooter, which she acquired after she gave up driving her car. She is also an avid reader.

Flo Robinson
1919 - 2000

During the 1970's and 1980's the city of Coventry gained a national reputation for pioneering work in the field of community education. The concept was not new - village schools together with the church had traditionally been the centres of communal activities, but increasingly schools had become isolated from the areas they served. Most schools remained closed during the holidays, evenings and weekends; teachers were held in awe, not always for the best of reasons; contact with parents was usually limited to an annual formal meeting, (unless there was a severe crisis) and many members of the community would admit that they remembered their own schooldays with distaste and often loathing. There was little accountability in the 20 years following the war, schools doing their own thing with seemingly little regard for those who provided the rates and taxes. Yet at the same time there were national and local reappraisals of the different aspects of education ranging from the 1973 -"Education - Framework for Expansion;" research into nursery education; the 1974 Halsey Report on Education Priority Areas; a review of teacher education and national and local reviews of the curriculum and the examination systems.

The time was ripe for new initiatives and Coventry took a positive step in setting up community education projects; establishing centres for changing the education opportunities of local communities based on local schools and answering their needs from nursery to adulthood. Community education was not just about opening and using the resources, which had after all been paid for by local communities. Nor was it just about accountability of the professionals towards their students and parents. It was all these things but it was also about acknowledging and advising that children made better progress academically, socially and emotionally when their parents were actively involved in the education process. The new community projects were based on several initiatives that had taken place in various schools but these had not been widespread and were often regarded with suspicion by local authorities and the teaching profession. In the project areas, schools were given community budgets and courses were organised, sports and other school facilities opened to the community; teachers visited homes; toy libraries and parent toddler groups were set up; above all parents were encouraged to come into schools and participate in the learning process.

One of the prime movers in this revolutionary thinking was Flo Robinson. Always known as Flo throughout the city, she was a tireless bundle of energy full of ideas and enthusiasm. She affected all who met her with her zest for life, her belief in the joys of education and her commitment to children and their families.

Flo grew up in Middlesborough with her grandparents in the house over and behind the general store that her grandmother ran. In addition to her share of household chores, Flo was expected to "do up" the books in the shop on a Friday night. She found reading, writing and adding up easy during her early years and realised much later what a great help it had been to be surrounded by the printed word. The shop itself was a community focus with the bench inside the door where shoppers sat to chat, and with Gran lending out the box of baby clothes or the boards and sheets for laying out the dead.

Flo won a scholarship to the local High School and at the age of 11 became the Kindergarten Sunday school teacher where her self-taught skill on the piano, playing hymns and songs by ear, was put to good use. The church at that time and in that area was the centre of the community. As she wrote in later life: "Church festivals gave a pattern to life. Church was a place where people cared. It opened doors to a love of music, to the language of the Bible and to the appreciation of beauty. It offered the opportunity to develop skills and lifelong friendships." She could have been writing about the primary school where later she was to put to use those talents and experiences, which the church had fostered and encouraged. It was the priests who persuaded Gran that Flo should go to training college ("She's a born teacher"), and without doubt, the debt that she felt she owed them and their active role in the community influenced her thinking towards the community aspect of school life that she came to believe was pivotal in education. Talking to children, telling stories and organising lessons and outings at Sunday School, were to be invaluable in Flo's later career.

Before she went to training college in Darlington (which was a huge event in the family where women especially did not go on to further education), Flo had very mixed experiences as an uncertificated teacher in a variety of elementary schools. It was in Grangetown in classes of 50 pupils that she witnessed the effects of grinding poverty on childrens' education and it was there too that she learned about the dedication of teaching staff. These experiences left a legacy that she never forgot, always surfacing in her drive to widen the horizons of children in such conditions and in her genuine admiration for and appreciation of teachers who shared her aim.

At college, Flo had the chance to develop her musical creative and dramatic skills. She helped friends who were struggling with learning to sight-sing tonic sol fa, spent hours in the evenings in the "Aladdin's cave" of an arts and crafts room and made a convincing St Joan in the college production of the play. She also roused the envy of her friends by her piano playing, "She could play all the tunes with both hands and no music." When she later became a teacher and then head teacher, she was many times able to quell restless classes by impromptu singing and playing.

Once Flo had gained her teacher's Certificate, she had the opportunity to work for several years in the nationally renowned Arthur Pearce Demonstration School in Darlington. The school set high standards of kindness and courtesy to children and of enjoyment in learning that Flo was to follow all her life. Her subsequent career packed in a variety of education experiences. Teaching in primary schools was followed by further qualifications at the London Institute of Education, joining the staff at Bedford Froebel College as an adviser on infant teaching methods and then becoming an adviser in Oxfordshire. Then came a gap when home and family took over. With her husband David and their two sons, Flo spent three years in Barbados, where David's job had brought them, an idyllic interlude where Flo was able to spend much time with their boys before they went to school. David, an engineer, then joined GEC in Coventry and the family settled in Balsall Common. While she was still young Flo was asked to go to help out in remedial studies at a secondary school. She found herself the only woman on the staff and very taken aback by the perception of her role. "At the weekly assembly, all the staff trooped on to the platform and I often spent time before assembly sewing on buttons because uniform had to be perfect or the boys would be in trouble."

Flo became a deputy and then a primary head teacher and this was the start of her community education involvement. It was during her years as head of Annie Osborn Primary School and later as teacher/adviser at Eburne Community Education Project that Flo's reputation was established as "one of the most remarkable educators it has ever been my privilege to meet." So wrote John Rennie, Coventry's Community Education Adviser, and later head of the Community Education Development Centre (a national agency, based in Coventry). The northeast area of the city, in which both Annies and Eburne were situated, covered some of its most disadvantaged areas, and in 1971, when she became head of Annies, Flo soon began to change things. She was determined to open the doors to parents and try to get them involved in their childrens' education. She knew that, unlike in her own childhood, very few families had a community aspect to their lives. Young mothers were often isolated, either as single parents or with partners at work, and extended families no longer the norm. Many young people had come to Coventry in the boom times of the mid-1960s when Coventry was one of the fastest growing cities in Europe; grandparents were often many miles away. As the 70s progressed, the boom receded and poverty was a serious problem in the housing estates of the area. Many parents also had undergone unhappy school experiences themselves, had little confidence in their own abilities and were uncomfortable in the presence of teachers. Flo wanted to change all that. She had a vision of the school as the centre of the community and she set about to make this happen.

Some of Flo's initiatives might seem commonplace in present primary schools but in the early 70's were almost revolutionary. She did not hesitate to use, adapt and adopt any measures which would make school more attractive to the community at large. Parents were actively encouraged to come into school she even sent letters signed "Love from Flo." There were social events, family assemblies, a parent/toddler group, a toy library, parenting classes and many visits to childrens' own homes. Staff who were at Annies during this period have a wealth of stories to tell the end of term parties for parents with food organised by the parents while Flo would be dancing in the middle singing "Viva España" at the top of her voice. She always said: "Many of these lasses have no fun in their lives they deserve to have a good time." Then there were the summer fairs which seemed to get bigger and bigger each year. David used to organise rides on a miniature train and their two boys would be there helping. There were bonfire night parties, where Flo's family organised splendid displays and food afterwards; there were the family assemblies where new babies were welcomed, where childrens' and parents' achievements were celebrated and where everyone's birthday was a special occasion. Above all, there was a breaking down of barriers between home and school. Parents knew they were welcome in their school, they could approach Flo and she would listen; they could talk to the teachers about their children and they would listen. They were encouraged to come into school to find out how and what the children were learning. Classes were organised for parents in basic skills, in parenting, in art and craft. Staff ran keep fit sessions in the evenings. If there were problems, Flo would visit their homes. Many a cup of tea was drunk on the estate while children were discussed and more often than not, parents' problems as well.

Flo was the first to admit that community education was a learning process for her too. Visiting homes opened her eyes to the problems families faced. She often returned to the school exhausted and upset, exhausted because she had been battling against bureaucracy, and upset, not by the parents but by the poverty she found and the injustice of the system. She was particularly moved once when she visited a child's home, because he was coming to school in a smelly state. Flo knew she had to use all her tact, and drawing on her own experience as a mum, she arrived with a bottle of bubble bath, which she said she found useful with her own boys when they wanted to avoid soap and water. The young mother thanked her for the kind thought but confessed that with a large family, hot baths were a luxury they could seldom afford. Flo was humbled by the episode but angry at the unfairness of it all.

One of her favourite expressions was: "These kids deserve a fair crack of the whip." On one occasion the school was visited by the whole Education Committee in the 1970's this was a way for committee members to keep in touch with what was going on in schools. The assembled guests barely got a word in Flo harangued them without pausing for breath, battling for resources and above all, staff for her children.

On another occasion, tired of the constant battle to get sufficient teachers each year, for at that time schools were not responsible for their staffing budgets she stormed down to the Education Office demanding to see the director who was out. Undaunted, she found a chair and sat outside his office until he returned, long after everyone else had gone home.

After nearly seven years as a primary head, Flo became the teacher/adviser for Eburne Community Education Project, which worked with 10 schools in the north east of the city, part of a web of five such centres covering Coventry's most disadvantaged areas. The move seemed a natural progression. She had laid firm foundations in her own school and was now to embark upon service to a wider community. The aim of the project was to help change the lives of local people, giving them a choice in educational activities which could in many cases mean a fresh start and new hope for the future. Flo's task now was to inspire and lead her group of 10 schools to take up the ideas that she had pioneered at Annies (and those which had been pioneered elsewhere in the city). These included many initiatives to stimulate literacy. Flo was convinced that literacy was the " window to the world", so classes were organised for parents to learn how to help their children. Because she knew that many parents had no confidence in their ability to share a book with their child (indeed, they told her so!) she and her colleagues organised "reading packs" to help parents; devised reading diaries for home school links; provided story boxes for homes where there was little money to buy books; and developed games and tapes to enhance the reading skills for both children and parents. As teacher/adviser, she supported and guided her colleagues in all the schools with her drive and determination. Not only parents but also teachers acknowledged the change that Flo's enthusiasm and new ideas brought to their lives and jobs.

One parent, who in future years was to go on to gain a university degree, wrote to Flo: "After years of isolation and depression, finally I found in your courses something my mind had been craving for. There was a reason to dress up and go out, there was something to talk about, and above all my confidence started flooding back. I began to read again. Now I am craving for knowledge, which at school I hated. To you, Flo, the biggest thankyou. I know you work hard to give people like me a second chance."

Another parent, who had returned to study, wrote, "I am one of those who started going to the Monday morning craft class. I thought that Monday morning was just for washing. Now I know that washing can dry as well on Tuesday or Wednesday. We have had such enjoyment from the lovely things we make. I'd thought I'd never be able to do it but I did."

John Rennie recalls how Flo was determined that parents who achieved exam results or certificates of attendance or proficiency, should have those achievements acknowledged and how she successfully persuaded the Director of Education to present certificates to mums who had never before received any award. The director himself paid tribute to Flo's role in pushing forward through the opening provided by the city's policy. He wrote to Flo on her retirement "the movement through the gate and the new pastures used, depend on the shepherds and the bolder spirits to lead and show the way through. You have done that so well with such warmth and enthusiasm."

Similarly, for teachers, Flo provided not only inspiration but also practical help and common sense. After a community education conference in Newcastle in 1981 a teacher wrote to Flo: "Thank you hardly expresses the admiration we all feel for your self-giving and the way you transmit enthusiasm, making things seem not only possible but natural." In Coventry Flo's help was always practical and down to earth. One head teacher expressed reservations about parents attending a function. Flo returned not only with printed publicity but also cups and saucers for refreshments.

During those years at Eburne, Flo's practical advice reached a far wider audience than the parents and teachers of the Eburne project. She broadcast regularly on the local radio station and set up education fairs and stalls in places like Asda, BHS and Owen Owen. Flo was in demand from other schools in the city both to talk about community education and to provide practical help in achieving it. She travelled widely to other education authorities to "spread the message" and she continued her abiding interest in early years education by becoming an executive member of the British Association for Early Child Education (BAECE).

After her retirement from Eburne, she worked for the Community Education Development Centre. Her energy was undiminished and she brought her great experience to help develop a number of C.E.D.C. projects in various parts of the country. After three years increasing ill health prevented her from travelling too much and eventually she was forced to retire. An accident left her housebound but did nothing to crush her spirit and enthusiasm for education. From her wheelchair, Flo wrote letters, researched on the internet, read widely and continued to influence and enthral her family and friends with her wisdom, experience and empathy with everyone. She influenced so many lives children, parents, friends and colleagues. Her love and concern for people coloured her whole life. Once Flo got to know someone, they and all her family became important to her. In those last years, she maintained a keen interest in the staff and parents at Annies and Eburne and greeted visitors with: "Tell me what's new."

Friends were often presented with clippings from newspapers or a recent book with: "Have you read this?" or: "What do you think of this?" She continued her research into early childrens' literature and became fascinated by her own family history, all the while taking immense pleasure and pride in her sons' achievements and the development of her adored grandchildren.

When Flo died in the summer of 2000 there was a huge gap in so many lives. Yet her funeral in Oxford, though tinged with sadness, was not a solemn affair. Many friends from all stages of Flo's life paid tribute to her and celebrated that they had been fortunate to know her and to have learned so much from her. Their lives and countless others had been enriched by her presence and by her work. Many colleagues can still vividly remember her standing in front of a packed hall at Annie's weekly family assemblies, probably with an arm around a child or a mum and leading the singing. A favourite song was:-

When I needed a neighbour
Were you there, were you there?
And the creed and the colour and the name won't matter
Were you there?

Wherever you travel
I'll be there, I'll be there
And the creed and the colour and the name won't matter
I'll be there

That was Flo.

With thanks to David Robinson, Sheila Karran, Pat Davies, John Rennie, Daniel Jonas, Paula Mozassari and Lillo Criminisi.

Margaret Rylatt

<u>Collections Research and Development Manager Herbert Art Gallery And Museum</u>

Margaret Rylatt, nee Sweeney, was born in Coventry in 1938. Her home was in Broomfield Place, but her parents having separated before her birth, Margaret spent much of her childhood with her grandparents in Lord Street, Chapelfields. Here, she was surrounded by many aunts and uncles. On her mother's remarriage Margaret eventually acquired two brothers and a sister as well as a very loving and supportive stepfather. She attended Spon Street Primary School and Hearsall Secondary Modern Girls' School leaving at the age of fifteen.

I remember my mother saying to a neighbour, "I don't know what Margaret will do, she's not going to work in a shop all the while". The neighbour said "Oh I think she will marry Tony H", a boy two days older than me. We'd been brought up together. I said I will <u>not</u> marry anyone round here that's for sure. I'm going to have a house. I'm going to have a car. I can hear the neighbour's reply now. "The trouble with your Margaret is she's too big for her boots, she thinks she's something she isn't".

Margaret married Barrie Rylatt when she was eighteen and had two sons. She is now divorced.

Her grandfather was a drayman working for the railway company and he frequently referred to Mr J.B. Shelton, the Coventry Antiquarian, who was also a drayman about whom Margaret later wrote a book.

I did lovely things with my grandfather, like helping him in the allotment, hence I love gardening. I still like digging and getting dirty. He used to bring his horse home at lunch time and as soon as he went grandma used to give me a bucket and shovel to go outside and pick up the horse droppings, to put up the garden near granddad's rhubarb. One of the earliest photographs I've got is of me is sitting in a wheelbarrow, which I have pushed all my life. We used to go for long walks across Hearsall Common and pick broom for grandma, and granddad talked to me all the time. He was a great influence in my life really. He introduced me to nature because he was a countryman and this is where I get my love of the countryside and the natural world.

Grandfather used to tell me things about old Coventry and Mr Shelton. That's where my love of history came from, but the one thing I didn't like about history was that there were never any Margaret Sweeneys around and I wanted to know about those people. I just felt they were so important. It was something I remember from history at school.

I went to the Bethel Church for a long time. I did everything, eventually teaching in the Sunday school. I quite liked it and then, when we began going to the 'grown-up' services, I started to analyse things. Archaeology is about analysing and drawing conclusions. So I stopped going, but it took a great big chunk out of my life.

Later while employed at Cash's, Margaret lived with an aunt and uncle in Blackwatch Road. Her uncle was a Catholic and although her aunt did not convert on marriage, their children were brought up in the faith. Margaret decided to attend St Elizabeth's church with her cousins. 'I liked the history and ceremony of it and I'd already thought about Henry VIII and the Dissolution. My history lessons all came back to me so I decided I'd take instruction'.

In the early years of their marriage Margaret and her husband both worked at Rootes car factory living, as they did then, at Ryton.

I decided I needed to do something with my life and stop flitting around, so I did a Pitman's shorthand and typing course. Then I got a job in Rootes as a flexi-writer operator. A flexi-writer was the forerunner of a computer.

I wanted a hobby to do with history, but didn't know what. I wasn't thinking about it seriously, I was just reading all the things I could. In those days my husband used to take *Punch* magazine and in it they used to have what was on at the British Museum every month. If there was a lecture on Egyptology I used to go to London on a Saturday just to this lecture. I did this for I don't remember how many years. So my first interest was Egyptology.

One day I read in the *Coventry Evening Telegraph* in about 1963 about the archaeologist Charmian Woodfield, who went on strike, because she was doing some work at Whitefriars and the corporation workmen were taking all the lead off the windows. I thought 'that's just a lady after my own heart'. I was just fascinated by this lady so I went to see her. I don't know what made me go, I just went and said I haven't done archaeology, but I would love to. I would be a millionaire now, if I only had 10p for every time someone has said that to me since. That's the one thing people say to you. Anyway, Charmian said 'well if you want to, come and do some work'.

It was just about that time that the Coventry Archaeological Society was being reformed and reconstituted. I joined this newly formed society Coventry and District Archaeological Society (CADAS). I'm one of the founder members of the new society and I think I've played every role, all but treasurer. I've been the chairman so many times. I have been secretary, I've been the events secretary and vice-chairman. I've been the chairman now for years. I try and pass it over every year, but nobody wants it. It's growing and its wonderful, because I'm doing my courses at university as well and all my students join, so I hope I'm involving the students in archaeology in a permanent way, rather than transient. I'm totally and absolutely involved with the society.

When Charmian left, Brian Hobley applied for her job and got it. As I was working for Charmian as a volunteer, I carried on working for Brian.

When I first started working at the museum as a volunteer, I was digging all summer out at the Lunt during the week. I needed to earn some money for many reasons. Next door but two to us was a man who was a franchised baker. He had his own bread round and he wanted to expand it. He delivered in Warwick and places like Hatton and he said to me. 'If I buy another van would you like to go and do this?' So I did. I just had a good time and I loved it. I just threw myself into it. By summer it was time to go back digging and I just threw myself into that.

We started at the Lunt in 1964 and I've been there since the first turf was taken up. My first dig was on the Priory and I'm back there now, the beginning and end of my career as an archaeologist. I worked as a volunteer for a couple of years, but again I cannot do anything by half. I had to go every day. Eventually Brian, having secured some funding, argued with the director that he needed an assistant and I got the job as the archaeological assistant. [1972]. It was advertised. I had no formal qualifications at that time, but mounds of experience.

What I did was to start doing two extra mural classes in the evenings, which in those days were run by Birmingham University. I did those for years and years. I did so many courses on the Roman army I could think like Caesar.

I like Roman military history and apart from that, the mediaeval period and monasticism. I love the twelfth, thirteenth and fourteenth centuries because this is the big time for building; I love these two periods. It's the Roman army, not the Roman period.

There were four monastic houses in the city and I have dug on every one. You see how my religious background helps with understanding? I think one's life is almost like a jigsaw and sometimes you can't put the pieces together, but when you get a certain age you start looking and see that was very relevant. So you see why I wouldn't change it. I think what I've done has been for a purpose. I have to say now, this might shock you, but I am a total and absolute non-believer, but understand those who are.

In 1973, Brian Hobley left and I applied for his job and got it. So now I'd become the City Archaeologist, still with no degree. I hadn't even got my 'A' Levels then, but some of the biggest names in archaeology, certainly in our area, like Dr Graham Webster, Dr Philip Rahtz and Professor Barker who, I'd worked with at Birmingham University, gave me really good references and I got the job. Graham Webster said 'she has done the equivalent of four degrees, but she's never had time to sit exams'. I became the City Archaeologist in 1974.

As I have said I always throw myself into everything. I was digging all week and at the weekends with the Archaeological Society. I think in ten years we only had that many Sundays off. When one is the chairman and City Archaeologist you have to do it.

I started thinking I ought to do something about qualifications so I did my English and History 'A' levels. I think I just did it for myself. By this time, of course, I wasn't doing any extra-mural classes so I could go in the evenings to Tile Hill

College. I continued working and have done some brilliant excavations in the city and they're published. I'm pleased about that. Then I didn't do anything else because I'd got a job, was a full-time mum with two children and a big house and a husband to take care of. I really didn't feel I could do a degree, I just didn't have the time.

Later I decided to do the BA in History and Archaeology and went to Birmingham University. I was also lecturing at the University of Warwick. I became a teaching fellow and because of that, and all the work I'd done, I was awarded my MA.

Archaeology is always a challenge. It's not knowing what survives. The Priory site at the moment [2001] is fabulous. The beautiful piece of wall painting is absolutely gorgeous, but I've gone off it now and on to the next thing. The learning process never stops.

Living in a man's world I always had to be a Jack Jill of all trades. When I came into archaeology along with the Brian Hobleys, we actually had to do everything. We had to dig, we had to write out reports, we had to draw and do our planning, do our photography, put the fences up, and empty the Elsan toilet. We had to do all of those things.

Archaeology has changed totally. Today, practitioners of archaeology seem to specialise. As a senior keeper of archaeology I wasn't desk bound. I've never been desk bound. I could have been, but I like the 'hands on' approach. That way you stay part of your team. When I first applied for my job there were hardly any women in archaeology. It was very much a man's world. That's why I was so shocked to get it, not because I didn't have a degree, but because I was a woman.

I have dug in some exotic places: I have dug in Israel. I was once asked to go and do some digging in Cyprus and more exotic, I went to dig in Turkey, in a place called Synop, with Warwick University. I was asked to go along to help the students. When we arrived, the curator said they'd found a church with mosaic pavings and asked if we could dig it because it was going to be destroyed. Stephen, who was in charge of the students, said 'I've got an archaeologist with me, but she's not here to do that. She's here to come and work on my site'. Anyway he asked me if I would do it. I'm talking about a Byzantine church with mosaic floors. I have never excavated a mosaic floor in my life, but methods and techniques are the same, providing your techniques are good. Apart from that I've studied archaeology and the history of archaeology and how Sir Mortimer [Wheeler] dug his sites and how the 'greats' all dug their sites. The history of archaeology is a terrifically interesting subject. Anyway I said I would do this.

They use a tool which is a bit like a mattock, but smaller. It's called a Chater and when I left they gave me one as a present. I loved that. I excavated the mosaic so I was there to see it taken up and I've now seen it, just on film, relaid in another place.

I wouldn't move from Coventry. Coventry is so important and I have travelled the world now. From a little girl who remembers going to Kenilworth thinking it was miles away, I've lectured right across the States, I did a coast to coast tour. I've been to Australia and New Zealand and I've been to Israel so many times I think I know it. My sister-in-law lived there, that was a good, cheap holiday for me. I just used to hop on a plane and go. I got to know the archaeologists there, I just used to ring them up and say 'Hello I'm here'.

I met Sir Mortimer Wheeler. He was the greatest. I met quite a lot of notables including Mick Aston. He and I go back a long time and when he came to do Time Team he said "I've known this woman for thirty-five years". It's lovely we studied Carthusians together. We kind of grew up together in archaeology. He's a better archaeologist than you see on Time Team. He is a great monastic person.

The introduction of metal detectors has created huge problems for archaeologists, but again I've worked with the Metal Detector Society. I've lectured to them and I've encouraged them to come in with their finds. All these things are important to me.

I know my mother was so proud of me and my achievements. When I got my MA she came to the cathedral. It was the last photo I had taken with her, my father and sons, in my cap and gown. She was really chuffed. That was in the August and she died in January.

There are things that I am proud of. These are the students that have come through me and are now 'up there' as professors and doctors.

I go through all the planning applications every week with the council to say whether there is an archaeological implication in an application. That's one of the things that I've done that I'm particularly proud of. I made archaeology an integral part of the planning procedure. That is quite an achievement, because now the archaeologist always gets the planning applications. Developers can't get approval unless I say. If there is an archaeological implication, because I know the city, I go through the plans very quickly and can say there's nothing there.

When I wrote *Archaeology and Redevelopment* that was a major achievement in the country, for that was held up as a model for other archaeologists in other cities. Today we now have something called PPG16 (Planning Policy Guidance) for archaeology, but we were doing that well before PPG16 came in.

What I have tried to do all my working life is to try and put history over to people the way I would like to have been taught. I try and make it exciting and I make it fun, because so much history is not fun and is boring and taught by boring people. I try to make it understandable and try and draw parallels from modern times so that people can understand. I try not to use jargon.

I can make it sound fun. I can make you laugh, but in reality it was a very hard struggle. It was a hard struggle bringing up the boys. My mum said I had a convenient memory. I can make the worst day you can imagine sound good fun. It is hard work. What people couldn't see on Time Team was that it was those weeks in February [2001] when it was 12 below. I had about six coats on and we were frozen and you are standing around for so long.

I once got buried chest high in a trench, excavating next to the DHSS building, and the sides collapsed on me. The digger driver put his bucket behind me and scooped me out. I left my shoe down there and we couldn't find it, so I had to go all the way back to the museum with one shoe. Actually I did the sensible thing and took it off and walked barefoot.

Because of reorganisation in the museum, I actually took retirement and I retired on 31st December 2000 and came back to work on 3rd January 2001 like everybody else. When the *Telegraph* reported 'Mrs Rylatt has come out of retirement' Mrs Rylatt never went into it. I am still working every day. I lecture in the evenings and I'm off with CADAS on a trip to Dorset at Easter.

Archaeology is a job for life. It is one of those things; how can you ever knock off? It's 52 weeks a year. It's 365 days a year. It's all your life. It's whatever you do. I dig my garden and I can't help picking a piece of pot up if I see it. I go out by car or train and I am looking at fields for signs of ridge and furrow. How can you not? You're always an archaeologist, you're never anything else. From the minute you wake up you just think of it. It's a way of life.

That's how things have gone really and I've loved every minute of it. I love Coventry. I've had a most interesting life, but I have worked hard.

A Harvest of History. The Life and Work of JB Shelton. (Shelton Memorial Committee)
Coventry: Archaeology & Development (Coventry City Council, 1981)

This is a transcript of an interview with Margaret Rylatt in April 2001.

Jessie Sadler

Jessie was born into the Lawrence family during the Boer War towards the end of 1900, at 21 Smithford Street, Coventry. She spent her early years living above the shop of Webb's the fruiterers with her family. Mr. Webb, a well known figure in the city and a councillor, owned several shops selling fruit, vegetables and flowers. When he was taken ill in 1898, he was nursed by Mrs. Cooper (Ma Cooper of City Arms fame). As he lay dying he extracted a promise from Jessie's father, to take care of his widow and five children. As Mr. Lawrence had a wife and eventually seven children of his own this was quite a burden, but he never complained and took his pledge very seriously, running the business for nineteen years to the benefit of the two families. Some of his last words when he died in 1917 were to the effect that he had kept his promise.

Jessie had a tough time growing up with three older sisters, who obviously resented having to look after their little sister, although they had a brother and two more sisters later. When she was four years old her sisters took her to the fair in Pool Meadow, but when they returned home they had forgotten her and left her there. When their mother enquired where Jessie was, they said she was still at the fair. Frantic with worry Mrs. Lawrence rushed to the fairground and fortunately found Jessie holding the hand of a strange woman. She informed Jessie's mother that she had seen the child wandering about, had taken her home and given her something to eat. She had just returned to see if anyone would come to claim her. Mrs. Lawrence must have experienced considerable relief at finding her daughter, although she never told Jessie's father about the incident.

Soon afterwards the doctor recommended that the family should move away from the crowded premises at Smithford Street to a healthier district on the edge of the city. They moved to a cottage in Hollyfast Lane, Coundon, two doors away from 'The Nugget' public house. Not only did they have a large garden of their own, but rented another plot on the other side of 'The Nugget'. A gardener was hired to keep them tidy and grow vegetables and flowers, which were viewed with admiration by the neighbours. It was while they lived there that Jessie first started school. The children had a mile and a half walk to Keresley School and undoubtedly Jessie was the slowest of the group of four sisters. Here she suffered again at the hands of her sisters, who were not always kind to her in their attempts to hurry her along. She remembers a good many smacks. It was the responsibility of the children to go to Allesley to collect the meat before they went to school, so inevitably they were always afraid of being late.

Schoolmasters and mistresses were very strict in those days. Jessie's oldest sister Nellie, was struck across the back with a cane by the schoolmaster, Mr Lowsby, because she was talking during a lesson. This caused her to develop St.

Vitus's dance, a condition which remained with her all her life. The doctor who treated her wanted her father to prosecute the schoolmaster, but he would not. This sort of incident illustrates how ordinary people were in great awe of those in authority.

Eventually the family moved back to the city centre, to Starley Road. The children then attended St. John's School at the bottom of Holyhead Road. The school was run by a formidable husband and wife team, Mr. and Mrs. Birch. Jessie was a rather timid child and found the teachers very intimidating, but her older sister Roxillana, named after an elderly friend of her mother, was a much bolder character. One day she was cheeky to her teacher, who had some trouble pronouncing her name. She complained that the teacher had called her oxo instead of her proper name. This earned her a caning, but it did not seem to bother her unduly. Her brother Tom, also received the cane from his teacher Miss Ward. His father's reaction on being told of the caning was to remark that he would twist her ear off. A few days later Miss Ward visited Webb's shop to buy some flowers and remarked to their father, "You are going to twist my ear off, are you?" which caused him great embarrassment, knowing his son had repeated his words. Jessie's most vivid memory of the school was a large clothes basket full of socks which Mrs. Birch brought out for them to darn. The quantity never seemed to diminish despite their efforts at darning, which were expected to be perfect.

Rose, another of Jessie's older sisters, was a famous swimmer in her day. She qualified for the Olympic games in 1916, but unfortunately the games were cancelled due to the war and she was unable to compete. By the time the next one came along she was married and no longer interested in competitive swimming. However, at her peak she was travelling far and wide, swimming in competitions under the directions of her trainer Jimmy Ward. Altogether she won 23 medals throughout her career. An incident occurred which involved Jessie, when Rose took her to the swimming baths one day. Whilst there Jessie had a fall and knocked her head, causing concussion. Rose, unaware of Jessie's condition kept hitting her and complaining of her slowness on the way home. When they arrived their mother asked Rose where Jessie was, as she had not appeared. Rose began complaining that Jessie was acting strangely and would not walk straight. They found her unconscious at the bottom of the stairs and the doctor was sent for. She remained in a coma for two days, but recovered and it obviously did no lasting damage.

After leaving school at fourteen, Jessie went to work in one of Webb's shops, as did her sisters. Everyone seemed to know everyone else in those days, the chief of police and the chief of the fire service were regular visitors to the shop. The better off people from the grand houses in the Quadrant and Warwick Row would come to Webb's for their produce. Angela Brazil, the writer of children's stories and her sister, a noted artist, would call in and place their order. Jessie found the sisters very timid and unassuming despite their fame. Even royalty came into the Smithford Street shop, when two princes were staying with Vernon Pugh, in Coventry. This shop was managed at the time by Roxillana, who was totally unfazed by the event. Deliveries from the shops were made by a horse-drawn van in the early years. The horse was kept at the back of 49 Starley Road when they lived there, but when they moved to 45 Starley Road, the horse could not understand the change of address. It continued to go to number 49 and several times tried to get down the entry, which caused a few problems.

The First World War had a profound effect on everyone and Jessie's family had their share of tragedy. Her sister Nellie wanted to marry Alfred Webb, but her father was opposed to the match, probably because he thought of him as one of his sons. However, he relented under pressure and gave his consent. Alfred was sent to France soon afterwards to fight in the trenches. His first leave was due and he and his fellow soldiers were marching towards the coast, when he was taken ill and moved to the side of the road. At that moment a shell came down and killed him. His widow threw herself into caring for wounded soldiers at the convalescent home next to Barr's Hill School, where she became friendly with Mrs. Miller of Coundon Court. They also made jam at the Glenn's sweet factory for the war effort. She eventually married again.

Two of Jessie's brothers-in-law lost a leg in the war and Jessie's own husband, who had been a stretcher bearer in the war, was wounded by a bullet in the elbow. The greatest tragedy the family suffered though was the death of their father at the beginning of 1917. The Webb's chain of fruiterers had to be sold and Mrs. Lawrence was given the Webb's market stall, which she managed until the Second World War.

Jessie married Robert Sadler in 1925, he was a cellist in a cinema orchestra. They moved to Dudley where he worked at the Empire picture house. Robert had relatives in Dudley, who were all musicians or singers. The orchestra accompanied the drama of the silent films. They moved to Bournemouth after a short while, where they remained for four happy years. Over the years Jessie watched many of the films to which Robert played the accompanying music, but on one occasion she missed a film called 'The Four Horsemen of the Apocalypse'. Disappointed to have missed it and wondering what it was all about she asked Robert to explain the plot. His terse reply was, that it was about four soldiers and that was as far as it went, she never found out any more. He and the rest of the orchestra were probably only interested in the music and the action was incidental.

While in Bournemouth Jessie's mother made a visit and they took her on an outing to Shell Bay one Sunday, Robert's only day off. As they relaxed on the sand sunning themselves, they were spellbound to hear what they thought was

Paul Robeson singing 'Old Man River', which came ever nearer. A boat appeared with the singer on board. It turned out to be the cornet player from the orchestra. He thought he would surprise them after hearing about their outing from Robert.

On another occasion they went to 'Chapman's Pool', a beauty spot near Bournemouth, where yellow iris's grew in profusion around the pool. Jessie stood on the spot where Marconi had sent his very first wireless message to America. Their idyll in Bournemouth came to an abrupt end when the whole orchestra was dismissed with the advent of the 'talkies'. They decided to return to Coventry and bought a house in Mayfield Road, Earlsdon, where Jessie still lives with her daughter and son-in-law.

Robert could no longer make a living from his cello playing, although he played in amateur orchestras, such as those at the Co-op and the GEC. The remuneration was so bad that after performing in concerts for a whole week at the College Theatre, he was paid with one hundred cigarettes. Mr. Kennedy the owner of the Astoria in Albany Rd asked him to perform Liszt's Liebestraum, a very long piece, rarely performed in full. He practised with dedication until perfect. He was billed as 'Robert Sadler, the Eminent Cellist' and completed the performance to rapturous applause and was congratulated by Mr. Kennedy in person. In recent years Jessie was listening to Hugh Scully's radio show when he introduced the piece with the comment that no one ever plays it all the way through. Jessie wanted to write and tell him that her husband had done just that. Unable to exist financially on his musical talent he went to work for the GEC where he remained for 25 years.

Throughout the Second World War Jessie, Robert and their young daughter Pat continued to live in Earlsdon. When raids were in progress they sheltered under the stairs, not realising just how vulnerable they were. Jessie had no faith in the public shelters and did not have an Anderson shelter, so there was no alternative. During the blitz their house was damaged by flying debris, when a piece of concrete came through the roof, but it was soon repaired. Both her mother's and her sister's homes in Queen Victoria Road were bombed, but her nephew was so concerned about the plight of the people in the Greyfriars Green shelter, that he carried buckets of water to them to relieve their thirst, for which they must have been profoundly grateful.

Over a long and happy life Jessie has a wealth of memories, especially of her family and early years. Apart from the few years away from Coventry, after her marriage, she has experienced a whole century of change in one city, which few are privileged to see.

Interview took place on 7th May 2000.
Mrs. Jessie Sadler passed away on the 17th September 2001 shortly before her 101st birthday.

KAY NEWSON formerly SWEENEY

Many old residential streets having been bulldozed to the ground, Coventry's ring road was built. One street however remained, Starley Road, this too faced demolition. A Compulsory Purchase order hung over it, but thanks to the determined effort of a small group of residents it was saved and became an attractive residential road once more. Among those residents was Kay Sweeney.

Kay was born in Sligo, Eire and worked in the Civil Service. She came to this country on marriage and continued working as a civil servant. After twenty years the marriage broke down and Kay left her husband taking with her their four children. The two oldest, Geraldine and Angela were in their teens. The younger children were Vincent aged fourteen and Stephanie four. Kay felt a great sense of relief to be free from her marriage, however:

> It took but a short time for me to realise I had swapped one hell for another. Can you imagine what it is like to be homeless, a mother with four children? In the summer of 1973 I found myself in that desperate predicament. I was a statistic with seven thousand others on a council waiting list. I suppose I was luckier than most homeless people. I had two thousand pounds in my possession.

The money was the residue left from the sale of her house.

The family was split up. The two oldest girls had been given the use of a one bed-roomed flat belonging to a friend of the family. Kay and the two youngest children lodged with another friend, neither situation was satisfactory. They desperately needed their own home together.

Kay approached Coventry City's Housing Department. She felt that 'The clerks seemed to be handpicked for their authoritarianism and the ability to say no with cool detachment'. Her name was put on the waiting list. Next she 'trudged through the city' calling at all the estate agencies, but without success. Her problem escalated when she arrived back at her friend's house to be told she had to leave immediately. The only place to go was to join her daughters in their flat, one bedroom or not. It was not satisfactory and the two older girls lost the freedom that they were enjoying, but there was no option.

Some months previously Kay had booked a caravan holiday for them all and they took this 'our last holiday as a complete family'. Which gave her a brief respite from her problems. Although she had lost weight and felt that her nerves were almost shattered her 'spirit kept control' which was just as well in view of future events.

Kay returned home refreshed to continue her search for a house. She was recommended to see a councillor, the relative of a colleague with whom she worked. Taking her daughter Geraldine, and Mick the owner of the flat, she went only to be left feeling 'desperate, depressed and defeated, and worst of all degraded'. Afterwards 'for the only time Kay broke down uncontrollably'. Never again was she to be thus used by councillors or anyone.

On her next visit to the housing offices Kay related her circumstances to the clerk who 'looked sad . . . the sadness in her eyes was for me. I had met a humane official'. What is more she was told of a property and was directed where to pick the keys up. Euphoric, Kay left the office. At the Estates Office she was told she should not have been given the key, but she could keep it. They must have realised getting the key back would have proved very difficult, Kay was a defiant and desperate woman. The official told her that the houses were to be demolished therefore only essential repairs would be carried out.

The property was 42 Starley Road, Coventry 'an isolated oasis in the heart of the city, . . . [which] consisted of houses of 'strong, solid, red brick'. Kay found the house and with difficulty opened the door. It was in an appalling condition throughout.

> I entered the living room. It was black, stygian black. The ceiling, walls and doors were black. A lone settee sat drunkenly in the centre of the room, slashed, its innards spilling out over the floor. I walked towards the kitchen. It was almost unbelievable. The black spotted lino on the floor was littered with broken glass, rice and jam. Carefully slithering over this domestic mayhem I made my way to the sink. There appeared to be at least a hundred bottles in the brown-stained sink. . . . Gingerly picking my steps I made my way out of the kitchen. Climbing the stairs I prepared myself for all eventualities. . . . Strange, despite this awful mess, my heart was soaring. I've got a house. I will make it a home for all of us.

To Kay's credit she did. The garden too was dark, due to large lime trees growing there and she vowed to make it colourful, but conditions in Starley Road were dire.

After moving in conditions began to deteriorate further and despite numerous telephone calls and letters to the council, still nothing was done. The empty properties only had pieces of tin blocking the doors, to keep out trespassers, consequently they were easily removed to admit the social misfits who readily took possession. Burglaries in the occupied houses occurred frequently and the fire brigade was called out regularly to deal with fires in the empty houses.

Following a particularly serious fire the residents talked about taking action and decided to get up a petition, to be presented publicly, asking the council to do basic repairs and board up the empty properties more securely. Their councillor failed to present the petition, but he had reckoned without Kay's determination. 'I was not putting up with any more nonsense from anybody. Nobody was going to plamas me (soften me up) any longer. Let battle commence'. What a protracted battle it proved to be.

Older residents wrote to me and thanked me for what I was trying to do. They spoke of how the street had deteriorated. Once it had been a lovely street with well kept houses. They had sat and watched helpless, as it fell into decline over the years when the ring road was built.

A week later another house went up in flames. The residents, angry and despairing, turned to Kay to find a solution to their problems. Throughout that night she lay and pondered until she remembered the charitable institution for the homeless, Shelter. The next day she rang them and the advice they gave led her to seek help from a local charity, the Coventry Workshop, which advised residents' groups. Their workers consisted of some professionally qualified people and three such workers immediately became involved with the Starley Road tenants.

After assessing the problems they first suggested that the residents set up an action group and form a committee. Kay felt that at last here was someone who was interested in them.

Having organised themselves as suggested, a meeting was arranged and held in a local church hall. All the Starley Road residents attended, along with the Coventry Workshop advisers and members of several other sympathetic organisations. Kay was elected chairperson and her daughter Geraldine, secretary. Although Kay had never before spoken in public she succeeded in instilling confidence in everyone and advised the audience to speak with a communal voice from then on. 'Our campaign had begun'.

Kay's house was given over to producing posters. Such activity brought everyone together, including the children. It was fun and 'Starley Road had taken on a new dimension'. The art work was put into the windows of their houses. The local press sent along a reporter who was told about the dire conditions the tenants had to endure, and a photograph was taken of the residents on the green at the bottom of the road. Publicity was much needed.

On 17th October 1977 the petition was presented to the Planning Committee and the City Architect called for a report on Starley Road. This initiated a hurried survey by the council. Meanwhile Kay and her committee produced a 'Resident's Option', for the street and surrounding area, detailing essential repairs and listing objectives and benefits to both residents and council. This was delivered by hand to the City Secretary's department. They also circulated every councillor with a letter stating the objectives of their campaign.

When the Planning Committee met in November, the City Architect summarised the case and recommended a twenty year 'lifing' for the road as a residential one. This decision had to be approved by the Housing Committee.

After this meeting Kay wrote to the local paper criticising the planners for building huge tower blocks and demolishing city centre housing, which caused social disruption and distress. She suggested that 'they had now seen the light, and Starley Road would be saved'. It was something Kay felt very strongly about. The second occasion on which Kay was invited to speak was at the monthly meeting of the Trades Council. 'To say I was nervous was an understatement. When I stood up my legs turned to jelly'. Nevertheless her speech was well received. After it the representative of the Electricians Union promised to test the electricity in her street. He kept his word and issued a damning report on his findings.

Unfortunately the residents' optimism following the City Architect's proposal was short lived. In December a report from the same department recommended to the Housing Committee the demolition of the Starley Road houses on economic grounds.

The Starley Road committee compiled their own report pointing out inaccuracies and assumptions in the council's statement. Kay also wrote a speech which she hoped to deliver personally to the Housing Committee at their December meeting. 'I felt I had to make my own personal plea to the council'. Permission was granted for her to do so and the committee listened, but the Lord Mayor suggested that Kay and her group were being manipulated by political ideologists. He added that 'Starley Road had the hallmark of other recent campaigns in the city, but was better organised'. They took that last remark as a compliment to their ability. In truth the group had refused help from such people, who caused them many problems, as they unsuccessfully attempted to become involved. The decision to demolish Starley Road was unchanged. Kay stood up and said 'If you demolish our street you will do it with us still in it'. Her anger knew no bounds.

There was disappointment when the *Coventry Evening Telegraph* failed to give prominence to the fact that a resident has spoken to the Housing Committee for fifteen minutes. It had been an unusual occurrence, but instead the Lord Mayor's comment on their being manipulated by political ideologists was front page news.

Irate, Kay and two others decided to confront the editor of the biased report. Gathering fellow residents along the way, like the Pied Piper, she went to the newspaper offices. Next day the paper reported how the defiant residents had fought to save their homes.

On 9th December 1978 notices to quit were served on all the tenants.

In an effort to intensify the campaign Kay rang every national newspaper giving a résumé of the problem, but did not receive any replies. Housing problems were not uncommon. She wrote a poem which she sent to Sir John Betjeman who replied saying he could not do much, but suggested writing to the MP and councillors. 'He wished us luck in our campaign. I shall always treasure that letter. His reply boosted our morale at a time when it was at a very low ebb'. A letter to Lord Goodman, who many years previously had made a strong plea to 'everyone . . . to pull out all the stops and help people in bad housing', was never acknowledged.

When Kay wrote her Christmas cards she included one to the Housing Director. The idea escalated and all the residents sent cards to every officer and councillor.

Many letters of support for the campaign appeared in the *Coventry Evening Telegraph* so it was decided to get up another petition to the council. The Saturday chosen to do this was bitterly cold as Kay and her helpers set up tables in the shopping precinct. Over three thousand five hundred Coventry citizens signed. Signatures from residents outside the boundary were unacceptable.

Some Starley Road residents had accepted the council's offer of rehousing, therefore it was a depleted force which went to the council meeting to see the latest petition presented by the local councillor. The matter was referred back to the Housing Committee for a full debate.

Reporters from both the local press and a Birmingham paper asked Kay what the next move by the group was to be. She replied 'We shall fight and we shall win'. Whether she really felt so confident is anybody's guess.

With only one month to go, before the Housing Committee met to make a final decision Kay racked her brains planning the next strategy. This was to be a huge demonstration in the Precinct on the following Saturday.

While the plans were being drawn up a member of the Coventry Workshop rang with hopeful news. A midlands Housing Corporation was interested in providing money to rehabilitate the houses, but this depended on the council rescinding the demolition order. An architect was to carry out a survey, to ensure the houses were within the cost limits laid down, and the residents would have to form a co-operative.

As a co-operative the tenants become landlords too, not owning their own homes, but paying rent from which a small sum, deducted weekly, is earmarked for repairs. The responsibility for running the street lies with a tenants' committee.

Kay said 'I felt so excited, so exhilarated'. She wrote to the council suggesting that 'demolition on economic grounds was no longer the case'. A call was received from a reporter from BBC Radio Birmingham asking her if she would give him an interview. This was to be her first taste of broadcasting, but it was not her last.

> There was so much to do and so little time. I wished I didn't have to go to work it seemed a waste of valuable time. My mind was obsessed with one subject, that of saving the road. In the evenings there was always work to be done. I sometimes wondered if life would ever again be normal.

At this point Kay was offered a 'small council house in a relatively good area'. The offer came too late. She said 'Had it come when my children and I were homeless, . . . my home was here, and here I was staying'.

In February Kay was informed that the demolition order had been rescinded. Joyfully she spread the good news which made headlines in the local press. A happy photograph of the residents also appeared. There was a proviso; they were given six months in which to form a co-operative.

As Kay was leaving the council meeting, at which the decision to suspend demolition was ratified, she was approached by the Director of Housing. He wanted to arrange a liaison meeting with the campaigners. Kay hoped that they could revert to a more normal way of life, 'but I was wrong, very wrong'. There was so much to be done and the days too short. The next phase was to form a co-operative.

In July, Kay was asked if she would consent to appear on BBC Television in a community programme entitled *Grapevine*. She agreed and filming took place in August. 'Nerves' took over once again. 'Not for the first time I wished I hadn't been chairperson of the co-operative'. Her daughter Geraldine, was also interviewed, and other residents were filmed and made brief comments about the street. The interviews had lasted thirty minutes, but when the programme was televised they were disappointed that their story had only been allotted the final five.

Once more it was a race against time and regular meetings were held, with everyone concerned helping the residents to achieve their aim of a co-operative. Kay was involved in all of them. One of the most productive was when the 'lifing' was extended to thirty years by the council.

Residents were chosen for the first phase of the rehabilitation scheme. Kay decided she would move to number 45 which would probably be included in the second phase. 'I needed to escape the mantle of darkness and shadows cast by those overpowering lime trees'.

Correspondence increased until there was a 'massive amount of paperwork' and Kay was finding it difficult to cope. The many documents, which had been meticulously filed, took up a great deal of space in her house. She considered the suggestion that she continue doing the development work full time, but decided against it because she still had two school aged children and needed the security of a permanent job. The post of Development Worker was filled by Mel Bird, a friend of the family, who had voluntarily helped the cause so was fully conversant with events. His office was to be in Kay's house, temporarily at least. Later, a suitable property was found and made habitable. When an Educational Worker was appointed he shared the office.

Kay and the committee members had to learn how co-operatives worked, and attended several courses on the subject. Evenings were taken up by educational film shows, for present and future members and any other interested organisations. Members of the committee were to be responsible for interviewing applicants for the available houses, thus they needed practice in the technique. Even so Kay admits, with some embarrassment, that the first applicant she recommended was known by other panel members to be totally unsuitable. She decided that she was no psychologist.

Starley Road was quite well known throughout the local area and Kay's public appearances increased. She spoke about the bitter campaign to get decent housing and the advantages of co-operatives. She is very disappointed that of several students, who first approached her about the issue, not one let her know the results of their work.

> Working full time outside the home, being a mother and housewife, taking part in selections, interviews and innumerable meetings, my time was very precious. I was prepared to sacrifice it for these keen students, but I felt quite disheartened that they didn't think it worth their while to come back and say "Thank you" whatever the outcome had been.

It was a wonderful day when tenders had been received and a builder chosen. Kay as chairperson and Flo Llewellyn, who had become secretary of the co-operative, signed the contract along with the architect.

In 1979 work started and Kay says 'I doubt if there was a happier human being in the whole universe than me that cold December morning'.

Kay was as busy as usual. The local paper wanted a photograph, the *Birmingham Post and Mail* asked her for a synopsis of the 'Starley Road Saga'. They also took photographs. A BBC Radio producer asked for an interview and once more Kay felt extremely nervous, for the interviewer was in Birmingham and Kay in the cathedral crypt. She vowed never to do such an interview again, it must be face to face.

In 1980 Kay was asked to speak to Open University students who were attending a summer school at Warwick University. She admits she had come a long way since 1977 and her appearance before Coventry Trades Council pleading for help in saving the houses.

On 17th March 1980 the first rehabilitated house, number twenty-five, was ready for occupation. An appropriate date given Kay's Irish background and that of the first occupants. Shamrock was much in evidence.

Kay decided to have a lie-in before the ceremony, but was awakened to be asked to appear on BBC Television. This time she felt quite at ease as the interviewer was Geoffrey Green and having seen him many times on the television, Kay felt she knew him. Later the Independent Television crew arrived with Anne Diamond to interview her.

A huge crowd turned up to the opening ceremony including Mr Wilson the MP, council members and representatives of all who had been involved in any way with the street. Even the 'beat bobby' was invited. Fittingly Kay was asked to cut the ribbon. Later they watched the television screening of the occasion.

For four years the campaign had waged, and Kay often threatened to drop the whole project, but she always believed in the rightness of the cause. She was well supported throughout by her family, the small, but faithful group of residents and many individuals. Various organisations too were extremely supportive, but the advice, encouragement and practical help given by the Coventry Workshop and Coventry Trades Council was incalculable. When things looked grim their encouragement had been invaluable. Their close relationship developed into friendships. However, Kay was the mainstay who was looked to for inspiration, especially in the early days when the Starley Road group faced such seemingly insurmountable obstacles. Her home became the venue for meetings, the painting of posters, interviews with the press or television and social occasions. Initially her house was also the office.

Despite the domestic upheaval, over the years, Kay's children were never neglected and all went on to higher education and successful careers.

As Kay wrote in her diary of events 'Time seemed interminable. On 15th May 1982 we opened our last house. Despite all the odds we achieved the impossible'.

In July 1980 Kay had remarried and she and her husband remained in Starley Road until 1988, when they left to fulfil a wish to live by the sea.

Thanks to Mel Bird for suggesting that Kay deserved recognition and Dave Sternberg for his recollections.

Kay kindly loaned her diary and other documents which was most appreciated.